Betty Crocker

Halloween
Cookbook

HOUGHTON MIFFLIN HARCOURT

BOSTON NEW YORK

General Mills

Editorial Director: Jeff Nowak

Publishing Manager: Christine Gray

Senior Editor: Diane Carlson

Food Editor: Andrea Bidwell

Recipe Development and Testing: Betty Crocker Kitchens

Photography: General Mills Photography Studios and Image Library

Photography and Food Styling: General Mills Image Library

Publisher: Natalie Chapman

Associate Publisher: Jessica Goodman

Executive Editor: Anne Ficklen

Editor: Adam Kowit

Senior Editorial Assistant: Heather Dabah

Senior Production Editor: Amy Zarkos

Cover Design: Suzanne Sunwoo

Interior Design: Tai Blanche

Layout: Indianapolis Composition Services

Manufacturing Manager: Kevin Watt

This book is printed on acid-free paper. ∞

Published by Houghton Mifflin Harcourt Publishing Company

Published simultaneously in Canada

For information about permission to reproduce selections from this book, write to Permissions, Houghton Mifflin Harcourt Publishing Company, 215 Park Avenue South, New York, New York 10003.

www.hmhco.com

Library of Congress Cataloging-in-Publication Data

Betty Crocker Halloween cookbook. -- 1st ed.
    p. cm.
  Includes index.
   ISBN 978-1-118-38894-5 (pbk.), ISBN 978-1-118-38895-2 (ebk), ISBN 978-1-118-38896-9 (ebk), ISBN 978-1-118-38897-6 (ebk)
 1. Halloween cooking. I. Crocker, Betty.
  TX739.2.H34B47 2012
  641.5'68--dc23
                                                    2012012318

Manufactured in the United States of America

DOC 10 9 8 7 6 5 4 3 2

4500539728

Cover photos (clockwise): Spiderweb Black Bean Burgers (page 64), Gingerbread Skeletons (page 160), Honey-Pumpkin Dessert Squares (page 176), Chocolate Whoopie Pies (page 172), Pear Ghosts (page 200), and Chilling Jack-o'-Lantern Smoothies (page 60)

The Betty Crocker Kitchens seal guarantees success in your kitchen. Every recipe has been tested in America's Most Trusted Kitchens™ to meet our high standards of reliability, easy preparation and great taste.

FIND MORE GREAT IDEAS AT
BettyCrocker.com

Dear Friends,

Celebrate Halloween with the kids this year! Full of spooktacular party tips, creative ways to reuse leftover candy and bewitchingly delicious recipes, this book will inspire the whole family to enjoy the fun of Halloween.

Put a chilling twist on your favorite drinks and serve guests Spooky Berry Shakes or Witches' Brew. Transform favorite appetizers like meatballs and fries into Cheese-Filled Eyeballs and Crusty Mummy Fingers. Even supper can send shivers down the spine of guests with creepy creations like Spiderweb Black Bean Burgers and Scary Slow-Cooked Chili. And don't forget the best part of Halloween—the treats! From Friendly Ghost Cupcakes to Chocolate Bat Cookies, there's no end to the spooks with your favorite sweets.

From drinks to desserts, the fun never ends when creating a Halloween menu sure to scare!

Warmly,

Betty Crocker

Contents

Planning a Fright Fest

Just because you're past trick-or-treating age doesn't mean you have to miss all the Halloween fun. Why not host a ghoulish gathering and scare up a little (adult) fun of your own?

Set the Stage

- Get things off to a scary start by setting a motion-activated device outside your front door to emit a witchy cackle, scream or other spooky sound effect when guests walk by.

- Create fake gravestones out of cardboard and prop them up in your yard.

- Visit craft stores for items such as hands, feet and bones. You can prop them up in your yard to look as if corpses are coming out of the ground.

- Set up a strobe light or fog machine for atmosphere.

Activities and Entertainment

- Try picking a theme to convince guests to wear costumes. Suggest they come dressed as their favorite movie character, hobby or celebrity. Offer prizes for "Best Costume" and/or "Most Clever."

- Rent a classic black-and-white horror movie such as *Creature from the Black Lagoon*, *Dracula* or *Frankenstein*. Have the movie playing in the background with the sound low.

- Place skulls, cobwebs and spiders in unexpected places such as the bathroom, kitchen shelves and on stairwells.

- Set up a "Boo Bar" and serve drinks with black-licorice straws. When appropriate, dip the rims of cocktail glasses in black or orange sugar.

Tabletop Tricks

- Keep your color scheme simple—orange and black food and decorations go a long way to set the mood.

- Fill clear glass vases and serving dishes with black licorice twists, orange jelly beans, candy corn and chocolate pumpkins.

- For a quick and easy centerpiece, place a small vase inside a larger one and fill the space between the two with orange jelly beans, black licorice twists and white jelly beans. Fill the small vase with water and a bouquet of orange gerbera daisies.

- Look for items to create height on the table such as candlesticks, pedestals and vases. Don't be afraid to mix glass and silver.

- Hollow out small pumpkins to use as flower vases. You can also cut a large rigid foam pumpkin in half and fill with ice for beverages.

Candy-Covered Popcorn

PREP TIME: 20 Minutes • **START TO FINISH: 20 Minutes** • **8 servings (1 cup)**

1 cup orange-colored vanilla candy melts

½ cup chocolate-flavored candy melts

8 cups popped microwave popcorn (from 6.5-oz. package)

1. In separate resealable freezer plastic bags, melt candy melts as directed on package.

2. Meanwhile, place 4 cups of the popcorn in ungreased 13x9-inch pan.

3. Cut small hole in 1 bottom corner of 1 bag. Squeeze bag to drizzle half of melted coating over popcorn; do not stir. Repeat with remaining bag of candy coating, using half of coating. Cover with remaining 4 cups popcorn. Drizzle with remaining coatings.

4. Refrigerate 10 minutes to set coating, or cool completely at room temperature for 20 minutes. Break into bite-size pieces.

1 Serving: Calories 230; Total Fat 13g (Saturated Fat 7g); Sodium 130mg; Total Carbohydrate 26g (Dietary Fiber 1g); Protein 2g **Exchanges:** ½ Starch, 1 Fruit, 1½ Other Carbohydrate, 2½ Fat **Carbohydrate Choices:** 2

Terrifying Tip

To melt candy melts, place in a resealable freezer plastic bag and microwave on Defrost for 1 minute. Squeeze the bag, then microwave on Defrost 30 seconds at a time, squeezing the bag in between, until melted.

Crunchy Peanut Butter Mix

PREP TIME: 25 Minutes • **START TO FINISH:** 25 Minutes • **20 servings**

4 **cups Golden Grahams®
cereal**

2 **cups Cocoa Puffs® cereal**

2 **cups thin pretzel sticks
(2¼ inch)**

1 **cup candy-coated peanut
butter pieces**

1 **cup dry-roasted peanuts**

10 **oz white chocolate baking
bars or squares, chopped**

2 **tablespoons butter or
margarine**

½ **cup powdered sugar**

1. In large bowl, mix cereals, pretzels, peanut butter candies and peanuts; set aside.

2. In 1-quart microwavable bowl, microwave white chocolate and butter uncovered on High about 1 minute, stirring once, until melted and chocolate can be stirred smooth. Pour over cereal mixture, stirring until evenly coated.

3. In large resealable food-storage plastic bag, toss half of the cereal mixture with ¼ cup of the powdered sugar until evenly coated. Spread on waxed paper to cool. Repeat with remaining cereal mixture and remaining ¼ cup powdered sugar. Store tightly covered at room temperature.

1 Serving: Calories 291; Total Fat 16g (Saturated Fat 6g); Sodium 219mg; Total Carbohydrate 32g (Dietary Fiber 2g); Protein 7g **Exchanges:** 1 Starch, 1 Other Carbohydrate, ½ High-Fat Meat, 2 Fat **Carbohydrate Choices:** 2

Terrifying Tip

For a festive look, fill snack-size plastic bags with this mix and secure with colorful Halloween ribbon.

Candy Corn Bark

PREP TIME: 10 Minutes • **START TO FINISH: 1 Hour 10 Minutes** • **36 servings (1 piece)**

24 oz vanilla-flavored candy coating (almond bark), chopped

2 cups broken thin pretzel sticks

2½ cups candy corn

1. Spray 15x10x1-inch pan with cooking spray. Line pan with waxed paper.

2. In large microwavable bowl, microwave candy coating on High 1 minute 15 seconds; stir. Continue microwaving and stirring in 15-second intervals until melted and smooth. Stir in pretzels and 2 cups of the candy corn. Spread mixture evenly in pan. Sprinkle remaining ½ cup candy corn evenly over top; press in lightly.

3. Let stand 1 hour or until completely cooled and set. Break into irregular 2- to 3-inch pieces. Store covered at room temperature.

1 Serving: Calories 155; Total Fat 5g (Saturated Fat 5g); Sodium 47mg; Total Carbohydrate 27g (Dietary Fiber 0.5g); Protein 0.5g **Exchanges:** 2 Other Carbohydrate, 1 Fat **Carbohydrate Choices:** 2

Terrifying Tip

If you have Halloween-themed cookie cutters, try cutting out shapes from this candy.

Roasted Pumpkin Seed Brittle

PREP TIME: 40 Minutes • **START TO FINISH: 1 Hour 10 Minutes** • **72 servings (1 piece)**

2 cups unsalted hulled raw pumpkin seeds (pepitas)

1 teaspoon vegetable oil

½ teaspoon salt

½ teaspoon paprika or smoked paprika

½ teaspoon ground allspice

1½ cups sugar

1 cup water

1 cup light corn syrup

2 tablespoons butter (do not use margarine)

1½ teaspoons baking soda

1. Heat oven to 400°F. In medium bowl, toss pumpkin seeds and oil until coated. Spread evenly in ungreased 15x10x1-inch pan. Bake 9 to 10 minutes or until golden brown. In same bowl, mix warm pumpkin seeds, salt, paprika and allspice. Set aside.

2. Grease 2 cookie sheets with butter. In 3-quart heavy saucepan, mix sugar, water and corn syrup. Cover; cook over medium heat 2 minutes. Cook uncovered over medium heat 25 to 30 minutes, stirring frequently, to 300°F on candy thermometer or until small amount of mixture dropped into cup of very cold water separates into hard, brittle threads. (Watch carefully so mixture does not burn.) Remove from heat. Add 2 tablespoons butter and the seasoned pumpkin seeds; stir until butter is melted. Immediately stir in baking soda.

3. Pour mixture onto cookie sheets and quickly spread to ¼ inch thick with buttered spatula. Cool completely. Break into pieces. Store tightly covered at room temperature.

1 Serving: Calories 61; Total Fat 3g Sodium 50mg; Total Carbohydrate 8g (Dietary Fiber 0.5g); Protein 1g **Exchanges:** ½ Other Carbohydrate, ½ Fat **Carbohydrate Choices:** ½

Terrifying Tip

The initial cooking step with the saucepan covered helps wash down sugar crystals from the sides of the pan and prevents crystallization in the resulting candy.

Bewitching Bites & Drinks

These wickedly good nibbles and potions will magically disappear in minutes.

Peppy Roasted Pumpkin Seeds

PREP TIME: 5 Minutes • **START TO FINISH: 35 Minutes** • **8 servings (2 tablespoons)**

1 **cup pumpkin seeds from fresh pumpkin**

2 **teaspoons oil**

2 **teaspoons taco seasoning mix (from 1-oz package)**

1. Heat oven to 350°F. Rinse pumpkin seeds; remove any pulp and fiber. Pat seeds dry with paper towels. Spread seeds in ungreased 15x10x1-inch pan. Drizzle with oil; stir to coat.

2. Bake 15 to 20 minutes, stirring once, until deep golden brown and crisp.

3. Sprinkle warm seeds with taco seasoning mix. Cool 10 minutes or until completely cooled before serving.

1 Serving: Calories 110; Total Fat 9g (Saturated Fat 2g); Sodium 50mg; Total Carbohydrate 4g (Dietary Fiber 1g); Protein 4g **Exchanges:** ½ Starch, ½ Other Carbohydrate, ½ Medium-Fat Meat, 1 Fat **Carbohydrate Choices:** 0

Terrifying Tip

For more pumpkin fun, pop these in the oven to roast while you carve your pumpkin.

Spiderweb Deviled Eggs

PREP TIME: 15 Minutes • **START TO FINISH: 2 Hours 40 Minutes** • **24 servings (1 deviled egg)**

2 teaspoons black gel or paste food color

12 eggs

6 tablespoons chipotle mayonnaise (from 12-oz bottle)

2 tablespoons sweet pickle relish

2 tablespoons finely chopped celery

⅛ teaspoon salt

⅛ teaspoon pepper

Chopped fresh chives

1. In 5-quart Dutch oven, mix 8 cups water and the food color. Place eggs in single layer. Cover; heat to boiling. Immediately remove from heat. Let stand 15 minutes. Using slotted spoon, transfer eggs, one at a time, to paper towels. Using handle of wooden spoon, tap each egg gently in several places. Transfer eggs to large bowl; cover with cooled cooking water. Refrigerate at least 2 hours.

2. Peel eggs; cut lengthwise in half. Slip out yolks into medium bowl; set egg whites aside. Mash yolks with fork until smooth. Stir in mayonnaise, relish, celery, salt and pepper until blended.

3. Mound or pipe egg yolk mixture into egg white halves. Garnish with chives. Serve, or cover and refrigerate.

1 Serving: Calories 60; Total Fat 5g (Saturated Fat 1g); Sodium 75mg; Total Carbohydrate 1g (Dietary Fiber 0g); Protein 3g **Exchanges:** ½ Medium-Fat Meat, ½ Fat **Carbohydrate Choices:** 0

Terrifying Tip

Wear gloves when preparing these spider-webbed eggs dyed in black-tinged water.

Crusty Mummy Fingers

PREP TIME: 15 Minutes • **START TO FINISH: 35 Minutes** • **8 servings**

2   lb sweet potatoes, peeled (about 2 large potatoes)

2   tablespoons water

2   egg whites

1   cup Italian style dry bread crumbs

¼   cup grated Parmesan cheese

½   teaspoon salt

½   teaspoon pepper

¼   teaspoon ground red pepper (cayenne)

    Cooking spray

1. Heat oven to 450°F. Spray 2 large cookie sheets with cooking spray.

2. Cut potatoes into 4x½-inch strips. In shallow dish, mix water and egg whites with wire whisk or fork. In another shallow dish, mix bread crumbs, cheese, salt, black pepper and red pepper. Working in batches, dip sweet potatoes into egg white mixture; roll in bread crumb mixture. Place potatoes in single layer on cookie sheets. Spray potatoes with cooking spray about 10 seconds.

3. Bake 18 to 20 minutes, turning after 10 minutes, until crisp.

1 Serving: Calories 140; Total Fat 2g (Saturated Fat 1g); Sodium 480mg; Total Carbohydrate 26g (Dietary Fiber 3g); Protein 5g **Exchanges:** 1½ Starch, ½ Fat **Carbohydrate Choices:** 2

Terrifying Tips

For a safe, easy way to slice sweet potatoes, cut a thin slice off the bottom of each potato before slicing so it will sit firmly on the cutting board.

Serve with ranch dressing for dipping.

Bugs in a Blanket

PREP TIME: 30 Minutes • **START TO FINISH: 45 Minutes** • **24 servings**

1 **can (11 oz) Pillsbury® refrigerated breadsticks**

24 **cocktail-size smoked link sausages (from 14-oz package)**

¾ **cup shoestring potatoes (from 1¾-oz can) or chow mein noodles**

Ketchup, barbecue sauce and/or mustard for decorating

Dip

1 **cup ranch dressing (from 16-oz bottle)**

1 **tablespoon ketchup**

1. Heat oven to 375°F. Unroll dough; separate at perforations into 12 breadsticks. With knife or kitchen scissors, cut each breadstick in half crosswise, making 24 pieces.

2. Wrap each piece of dough around center of each sausage, pinching to seal and leaving each end of sausage showing. Place seam side down and ½ inch apart on ungreased large cookie sheet.

3. Bake 11 to 14 minutes or until golden brown. Immediately remove from cookie sheet; place on serving plate or tray. Cool 2 minutes.

4. Insert shoestring potatoes into baked dough to resemble legs and antennae. Decorate "bugs" with dots or stripes of ketchup.

5. Spread dressing in 9-inch glass pie plate or on dinner plate. Spoon ketchup into small resealable food-storage plastic bag. Seal bag and cut tiny hole in bottom corner. Squeeze bag to draw a coil of ketchup over ranch dressing. Drag toothpick through coil from center out, creating a web. Serve dip with "bugs."

1 Serving: Calories 140; Total Fat 11g (Saturated Fat 3g); Sodium 360mg; Total Carbohydrate 8g (Dietary Fiber 0g); Protein 3g **Exchanges:** ½ Starch, 2 Fat **Carbohydrate Choices:** ½

Terrifying Tip

Kids will have fun helping "paint" these "bugs."

Halloweenies with Mustard Dip

PREP TIME: 20 Minutes • **START TO FINISH: 40 Minutes** •

44 servings (1 wrapped sausage and 1 teaspoon dip)

1 can (8 oz) Pillsbury® Crescent Recipe Creations® refrigerated seamless dough sheet

44 cocktail-size smoked link sausages (from a 1-lb package)

½ cup creamy Dijon mustard

1 tablespoon dried oregano leaves

1. Heat oven to 375°F. Line 2 (15x10x1-inch) pans with cooking parchment paper.

2. On work surface, roll dough sheet to 14x11-inch rectangle. Cut vertically to make 2 (11x7-inch) rectangles. Cut crosswise into total of 44 (7x½-inch) strips. Pat sausages dry with paper towels.

3. Wrap 1 strip of dough around each sausage to look like a little mummy; press firmly at each end to secure. Place 2 inches apart on pans for even browning.

4. Bake 15 to 20 minutes or until golden brown. Meanwhile, in small bowl, mix mustard and oregano. Serve warm sausages with mustard dip.

1 Serving: Calories 45; Total Fat 3.5g (Saturated Fat 1g); Sodium 190mg; Total Carbohydrate 2g (Dietary Fiber 0g); Protein 1g **Exchanges:** 1 Fat **Carbohydrate Choices:** 0

Terrifying Tips

Instead of using a refrigerated seamless dough sheet, try rolling these little weenies in puff pastry.

Short on time? Skip making the dip and serve with ketchup and/or regular mustard.

Mummy Toes

24 **cocktail-size hot dogs**

1 **can (11.5 oz) Pillsbury® refrigerated garlic breadsticks**

2 **tablespoons cheese and salsa dip or ketchup**

24 **sliced almonds, if desired**

1. Heat oven to 375°F. Cut a wedge into the end of each cocktail hot dog to look like toenail. Unroll dough; separate at perforations into 8 breadsticks. With knife or kitchen scissors, cut each breadstick into thirds, making 24 pieces. Wrap 1 piece of dough around each hot dog to edge of toenail. Place seam side down on ungreased cookie sheet.

2. Bake 10 to 12 minutes or until golden brown. Cool 3 minutes. Fill each toenail with ¼ teaspoon dip or ketchup. Insert almond to look like toenail. Serve warm.

1 Serving: Calories 160; Total Fat 10g (Saturated Fat 3g); Sodium 490mg; Total Carbohydrate 13g (Dietary Fiber 0g); Protein 4g **Exchanges:** ½ Starch, ½ Other Carbohydrate, ½ High-Fat Meat, 1 Fat **Carbohydrate Choices:** 1

Terrifying Tips

Make and refrigerate these snacks 2 hours before you want to bake them.

To easily fill the toenails with dip or ketchup, use a resealable food-storage plastic bag with the corner snipped off.

Cheese-Filled Eyeballs

PREP TIME: 20 Minutes • **START TO FINISH: 45 Minutes** •

48 servings (1 meatball and 1 tablespoon sauce)

2   lb ground beef round

1   cup Italian style dry bread crumbs

½   teaspoon salt

½   teaspoon pepper

3   eggs, slightly beaten

8   sticks (1 oz each) string cheese

1   can (2¼ oz) sliced ripe olives, drained

1   jar (24 oz) marinara sauce, heated

1. Heat oven to 375°F. Spray 2 (15x10x1-inch) pans with cooking spray. In large bowl, mix beef, bread crumbs, salt, pepper and eggs. Shape into 48 (1-inch) balls. Place in pans.

2. Cut each cheese stick into 6 pieces. Gently press a piece of cheese into each meatball.

3. Bake uncovered 20 to 25 minutes or until meatballs are thoroughly cooked and no longer pink in center. Place olive slice over cheese on each meatball. Serve with warm marinara sauce for dipping.

1 Serving: Calories 67; Total Fat 3g (Saturated Fat 1.5g); Sodium 192mg; Total Carbohydrate 3g (Dietary Fiber 0.5g); Protein 6g **Exchanges:** 1 Very Lean Meat **Carbohydrate Choices:** 0

Terrifying Tip

Use a 1-inch cookie scoop to ensure evenly sized meatballs.

Wart-Topped Quesadilla Wedges

PREP TIME: 10 Minutes • **START TO FINISH:** 30 Minutes • **8 servings (2 wedges)**

4 **flour tortillas (8 inch; from 11.5-oz package)**

½ **cup refrigerated original barbecue sauce with shredded pork (from 18-oz container)**

2 **teaspoons sweet pickle relish**

½ **cup shredded American-Cheddar cheese blend (2 oz)**

Cooking spray

4 **teaspoons shredded American-Cheddar cheese blend**

8 **pitted large green or ripe olives, cut in half lengthwise**

1. Heat oven to 375°F. Spray cookie sheet with cooking spray. Place 2 tortillas on cookie sheet. Spread ¼ cup barbecue sauce with pork over each tortilla. Sprinkle each with 1 teaspoon pickle relish and ¼ cup cheese. Top each with second tortilla. Spray tops with cooking spray.

2. Bake 10 to 12 minutes or until tortillas are lightly browned and filling is hot.

3. Remove partially baked quesadillas from oven. Immediately drop 4 teaspoons cheese by ¼ teaspoonfuls around edges of quesadillas, spacing evenly and making 8 piles of cheese on each. Top each pile of cheese with 1 olive half to look like wart.

4. Bake about 1 minute longer or until cheese is melted. Let stand 5 minutes before serving. Cut each quesadilla into 8 wedges.

1 Serving: Calories 120; Total Fat 5g (Saturated Fat 2g); Sodium 350mg; Total Carbohydrate 14g (Dietary Fiber 0g); Protein 5g **Exchanges:** ½ Starch, ½ Other Carbohydrate, ½ Medium-Fat Meat, ½ Fat **Carbohydrate Choices:** 1

Terrifying Tip

Assemble the quesadillas up to an hour ahead of time. Cover and refrigerate until ready to bake.

Cheese Pumpkins

PREP TIME: 15 Minutes • **START TO FINISH: 30 Minutes** • **8 servings (1 pumpkin)**

8 tablespoons smoky Cheddar cold-pack cheese food (from 8-oz container), well chilled

2 teaspoons finely chopped peanuts

4 butter-flavored pretzel spindles or sticks, broken in half

16 tiny pieces fresh parsley leaves

1. Line small serving plate with waxed paper. Roll each tablespoon cold-pack cheese food into a ball; place on plate. Refrigerate 10 to 15 minutes for easier handling.

2. With end of toothpick, draw ridges around balls to look like pumpkins. Dip bottoms of cheese balls in chopped peanuts.

3. Just before serving, insert 1 pretzel half into each pumpkin for stem. Add parsley for leaves. Store in refrigerator.

1 Serving: Calories 50; Total Fat 4g (Saturated Fat 2g); Sodium 120mg; Total Carbohydrate 0g (Dietary Fiber 0g); Protein 3g **Exchanges:** ½ High-Fat Meat **Carbohydrate Choices:** 0

Terrifying Tips

Turn the pumpkin making into a family affair! Have one person roll the cheese into balls and another shape the balls into pumpkins, while someone else can dip the pumpkins in peanuts and insert the pretzels. It's easy to double the recipe, so make as many as you'd like!

The texture or firmness of cold-pack cheese food can vary by brand. For these pumpkins, look for one with a firmer texture.

Savory Bat Wing Truffles

PREP TIME: 25 Minutes   •   **START TO FINISH: 25 Minutes**   •   **14 servings (1 truffle)**

8   oz chèvre (goat) cheese, crumbled (1 cup)

1   container (4 oz) garlic-and-herbs spreadable cheese

¼   cup basil pesto or sun-dried tomato pesto

1   bag (9.5 oz) blue corn tortilla chips

Thin pretzel sticks, broken

½   cup sliced pitted ripe or green olives

1. In medium bowl, mix cheeses and pesto. Shape mixture into 14 (1½-inch) balls.

2. In resealable food-storage plastic bag, place 4 cups of the tortilla chips; seal bag. Finely crush chips with rolling pin or flat side of meat mallet. Pour crumbs onto plate.

3. Roll cheese balls in crumbs, coating completely. Press 2 pretzel pieces into each truffle for eyes; place olive slices on pretzels. Just before serving, insert 2 tortilla chips on either side of eyes to look like bat wings.

1 Serving: Calories 179; Total Fat 11g (Saturated Fat 5g); Sodium 295mg; Total Carbohydrate 16g (Dietary Fiber 2g); Protein 6g **Exchanges:** 1 Starch, ½ High-Fat Meat, 1 Fat **Carbohydrate Choices:** 1

Terrifying Tip

Leave off the decorative chips and olive eyes as the final touch, and make these delicious first-course cheese truffles for any holiday occasion.

Warm Brie Jack-o'-Lantern

PREP TIME: 10 Minutes • **START TO FINISH: 20 Minutes** •

12 servings (2 apple slices, 2 crackers, and ¹⁄₁₂ round)

1 round (8 oz) Brie cheese

1 tablespoon apricot spreadable fruit

2 medium apples, each cut into 12 slices

24 round buttery crackers (about 3.5 oz)

½ cup apricot spreadable fruit

1. Heat oven to 350°F. Line small cookie sheet with cooking parchment paper or foil. With small knife, carefully cut jack-o'-lantern face in top of Brie, gently removing white rind and some of the cheese from under cuts to reveal face.

2. Using small spoon, spoon 1 tablespoon apricot spreadable fruit into cutouts of face. Place Brie on cookie sheet.

3. Bake 8 to 10 minutes or until sides feel soft and cheese is warm. Serve with apples, crackers and ½ cup apricot spreadable fruit.

1 Serving: Calories 140; Total Fat 7g (Saturated Fat 3.5g); Sodium 170mg; Total Carbohydrate 16g (Dietary Fiber 2g); Protein 4g **Exchanges:** 1 Starch, 1½ Fat **Carbohydrate Choices:** 1

Terrifying Tips

We suggest serving this dip with apple slices, but it tastes great with pear slices, too.

The white coating, or rind, covering Brie is edible. When heated, the rich, buttery cheese becomes very soft and spreadable.

Graveyard Bones with Dip

PREP TIME: 10 Minutes • **START TO FINISH: 35 Minutes** •
12 servings (2 tablespoons dip and 1 breadstick each)

1 can (11 oz) Pillsbury®
refrigerated breadsticks

1 egg white, beaten

2 tablespoons grated
Parmesan cheese

1 teaspoon dried basil
leaves

1 can (15 oz) pizza sauce,
heated

1. Heat oven to 375°F. Spray cookie sheet with cooking spray. Unroll dough; separate at perforations into 12 breadsticks. Roll each until 12 inches long. Loosely tie knot in both ends of each breadstick; place on cookie sheet (do not twist).

2. Brush breadsticks with egg white. Sprinkle with cheese and basil.

3. Bake 12 to 14 minutes or until golden brown. Serve warm "bones" with warm pizza sauce for dipping.

1 Serving: Calories 105; Total Fat 3g (Saturated Fat 1g); Sodium 380mg; Total Carbohydrate 15g (Dietary Fiber 0g); Protein 4g **Exchanges:** 1 Starch, ½ Fat **Carbohydrate Choices:** 1

Terrifying Tip

For younger kids, make shorter "bones" that are easier for them to handle by cutting the breadstick dough strips in half before tying knots in the ends.

Witches' Brooms and Sauce

PREP TIME: 20 Minutes • **START TO FINISH: 35 Minutes** • **32 appetizers**

1 can (8 oz) Pillsbury® refrigerated garlic breadsticks

1 tablespoon olive oil

⅓ cup grated Parmesan cheese

2 cups marinara sauce

1. Heat oven to 350°F. Spray 2 cookie sheets with cooking spray.

2. Unroll breadstick dough on work surface. Cut dough in half crosswise, and separate to make 16 strips; cut each of the strips in half lengthwise to make 32 thin strips. Place strips on cookie sheets, 1 inch apart. Using a small paring knife or kitchen scissors, make 4 thin cuts (2 inches long) on 1 end of each strip. Spread out cut ends to make bristles of each broom. Brush dough with oil; sprinkle with Parmesan cheese.

3. Bake 10 to 12 minutes or until golden brown. Serve with marinara sauce.

1 Appetizer: Calories 50; Total Fat 2.5g (Saturated Fat 0.5g); Sodium 170mg; Total Carbohydrate 6g (Dietary Fiber 0g, Sugars 2g); Protein 1g **Exchanges:** ½ Starch, ½ Fat **Carbohydrate Choices:** ½

Terrifying Tips

Serve these brooms with Scary Slow-Cooked Chili
(see page 86).

For easy cleanup, cover the cookie sheet with cooking
parchment paper.

Black Cat Canapés

PREP TIME: 30 Minutes • **START TO FINISH: 30 Minutes** • **30 appetizers**

30 slices (½ inch thick) white, rye or pumpernickel bread

Olive oil cooking spray

1 large clove garlic, finely chopped

1 cup pitted kalamata olives, drained, patted dry with paper towel, finely chopped

1 tablespoon extra-virgin olive oil

1 teaspoon lemon juice

⅛ teaspoon pepper

1. Heat oven to 400°F. Line 2 cookie sheets with cooking parchment paper or foil. Cut 30 cat shapes out of bread using 2½- to 3-inch cat-shaped cookie cutter. (Discard or save excess bread for another use.) Place bread cats on cookie sheets. Spray with cooking spray; turn over. Spray other side with cooking spray.

2. Bake 3 to 4 minutes, turning once, until light golden brown. Cool 5 minutes.

3. Meanwhile, in medium bowl, mix garlic, olives, olive oil, lemon juice and pepper.

4. Serve toasted bread with olive dip.

1 Appetizer: Calories 170; Total Fat 3.5g (Saturated Fat 0.5g); Sodium 430mg; Total Carbohydrate 29g (Dietary Fiber 1g); Protein 4g **Exchanges:** 1½ Starch, ½ Other Carbohydrate, ½ Fat **Carbohydrate Choices:** 2

Terrifying Tip

For a shortcut, substitute ⅔ cup purchased ripe olive tapenade in place of the ingredients in step 3.

Scarecrow-d Taco Dip

PREP TIME: 15 Minutes • **START TO FINISH:** 15 Minutes • **16 servings**

1   **package (8 oz) cream cheese, softened**

2   **teaspoons taco seasoning mix (from 1-oz package)**

½   **cup chunky style salsa**

¼   **cup sliced ripe olives**

1   **cup shredded Cheddar cheese (4 oz)**

1   **cup traditional refried beans (from 16-oz can)**

1   **cup chopped lettuce**

2   **cherry tomatoes**

     Triangular-shaped tortilla chips (about 3 inch)

1. In small bowl, mix cream cheese and taco seasoning mix until smooth. Spread on 10-inch plate. Spoon salsa evenly over cream cheese mixture. Reserve 4 olive slices; sprinkle remaining olives over salsa. Reserve ¼ cup cheese; sprinkle remaining cheese over olives. Spoon beans in center of plate; spread to 6-inch circle to resemble head of scarecrow. Sprinkle lettuce around beans.

2. Cut 1 tomato in half; place each half on scarecrow, cut side up, to resemble eyes. Add remaining tomato to resemble nose. Place 1 reserved olive slice on each "eye" to resemble pupil. Cut the remaining reserved olive slices in half and arrange the pieces to resemble mouth.

3. Arrange tortilla chips to resemble a hat on the scarecrow's head. Arrange the reserved cheese to come out from under the hat and at the bottom of the face to resemble straw. Serve dip with tortilla chips. Store dip in refrigerator.

1 Serving: Calories 110; Total Fat 8g (Saturated Fat 4.5g); Sodium 280mg; Total Carbohydrate 5g (Dietary Fiber 0g); Protein 4g **Exchanges:** ½ Other Carbohydrate, ½ Very Lean Meat, 1½ Fat **Carbohydrate Choices:** ½

Terrifying Tip

This dip can be made several hours ahead. Add the "hat" just before serving.

Pumpkin-Spice Spread

PREP TIME: 20 Minutes • **START TO FINISH:** 20 Minutes • **24 servings (about 1 tablespoon)**

1 **package (8 oz) cream cheese, softened**

½ **cup canned pumpkin (not pumpkin pie mix)**

½ **teaspoon ground cinnamon**

¼ **teaspoon ground nutmeg**

¼ **teaspoon salt**

¼ **cup chopped pecans, toasted**

10 **pecan halves**

1. In medium bowl, beat cream cheese and pumpkin with electric mixer on medium speed until smooth and creamy. Stir in cinnamon, nutmeg, salt and chopped pecans.

2. Spread cheese mixture on serving plate or in ungreased 9-inch glass pie plate. Cut 3 pecans in half lengthwise and position 3 pieces for each eye; arrange 5 pecans for mouth and 1 pecan for nose. Place remaining pecan on top for stem. Serve immediately, or cover and refrigerate up to 24 hours.

1 Serving: Calories 50; Total Fat 5g (Saturated Fat 2g); Sodium 55mg; Total Carbohydrate 1g (Dietary Fiber 0g); Protein 0g **Exchanges:** 1 Fat **Carbohydrate Choices:** 0

Bat Wing Dippers

PREP TIME: 15 Minutes • **START TO FINISH:** 40 Minutes • **24 bat wings**

4 **flour tortillas (8 inch; from 11.5-oz package)**

Cooking spray

1. Heat oven to 350°F.

2. With bat-shaped cookie cutter or kitchen scissors, cut tortillas into bat shapes. Place shapes and large scraps on ungreased cookie sheets. Spray both sides of shapes and scraps with cooking spray.

3. Bake 8 to 10 minutes or until golden brown and crisp. Cool completely, about 15 minutes. Serve as dippers for dips.

1 Bat Wing: Calories 25; Total Fat 1g (Saturated Fat 0g); Sodium 50mg; Total Carbohydrate 3g (Dietary Fiber 0g); Protein 0g **Exchanges:** ½ Fat **Carbohydrate Choices:** 0

Spider Bites

PREP TIME: **10 Minutes** • START TO FINISH: **1 Hour 30 Minutes** • **16 servings (1 shooter)**

Black Layer

- 2 envelopes unflavored gelatin
- 1 cup cold water
- ½ cup sweetened condensed milk (not evaporated)
- ¼ teaspoon black gel food color
- 1 tablespoon anise-flavored liqueur, if desired

Orange Layer

- 1 envelope unflavored gelatin
- 1 cup cold water
- 1 box (4-serving size) orange-flavored gelatin
- 2 tablespoons orange-flavored liqueur, if desired
- 16 gummy spider candies

1. Lightly spray 8-inch square (2-quart) glass baking dish with cooking spray.

2. In 1-quart saucepan, sprinkle 2 envelopes gelatin on 1 cup cold water to soften; heat over low heat, stirring constantly, until gelatin is dissolved. Remove from heat; stir in condensed milk, black food color and anise-flavored liqueur. Pour mixture into baking dish. Refrigerate 30 to 45 minutes or until set.

3. Meanwhile, in 1-quart saucepan, sprinkle 1 envelope gelatin on 1 cup cold water to soften; heat over low heat, stirring constantly, until gelatin is dissolved. Add orange-flavored gelatin; whisk until dissolved. Stir in orange-flavored liqueur. Remove from heat. Cool about 20 minutes, stirring occasionally.

4. Pour orange gelatin over black gelatin layer; refrigerate 5 minutes. Place spider candies in 4 by 4 pattern over partially set orange-flavored gelatin so each square will have a spider in center when cut. Refrigerate 30 minutes or until set.

5. To unmold, run knife around edges of gelatin to loosen; place cutting board over dish and invert. Remove dish. Place another cutting board over gelatin and invert again. Cut into 4 rows by 4 rows.

1 Serving: Calories 98; Total Fat 1g (Saturated Fat 1g); Sodium 46mg; Total Carbohydrate 17g (Dietary Fiber 0g); Protein 6g **Exchanges:** 1 Other Carbohydrate **Carbohydrate Choices:** 1

Terrifying Tip

Use different gummy shapes and gelatin flavors for other holidays.

Bubbly Black Punch with Wormy Ice Ring

PREP TIME: 10 Minutes • **START TO FINISH: 6 Hours 10 Minutes** • **16 servings (¾ cup each)**

1 cup gummy worm candies

4 cups green berry rush kiwi-strawberry fruit punch (from 128-oz container)

2 cans (12 oz each) orange carbonated beverage

2 cans (12 oz each) grape carbonated beverage

1 can (11.5 oz) frozen grape juice concentrate, thawed

3 cans (12 oz each) sparkling mineral water

1. In bottom of 6-cup ring mold, scatter most of candy worms. Pour fruit punch over candy, filling to within 1 inch of top (candy worms will float to top). Place remaining candy worms over edge of mold. Freeze 5 to 6 hours or until solid.

2. Just before serving, in 3-quart or larger punch bowl, mix carbonated beverages, thawed juice concentrate and mineral water.

3. Dip outside of ring mold in hot water until ice ring is loosened. Remove ice ring; place in punch so gummy worms are visible.

1 Serving: Calories 110; Total Fat 0g (Saturated Fat 0g); Sodium 35mg; Total Carbohydrate 26g (Dietary Fiber 0g); Protein 0g **Exchanges:** 1½ Other Carbohydrate **Carbohydrate Choices:** 2

Terrifying Tip

To get a head start, make the ice ring up to a week before your party.

Witches' Brew

PREP TIME: 5 Minutes • **START TO FINISH: 5 Minutes** • **16 servings**

1 quart lime sherbet, slightly softened

1 can (12 oz) frozen limeade concentrate, thawed

1 bottle (1 liter) ginger ale (4½ cups), chilled

Gummy worm candies, if desired

Lime slices, if desired

1. In punch bowl or pitcher, mix sherbet, limeade and ginger ale.

2. Ladle or pour into glasses. Garnish each serving with candy and lime slice.

1 Serving: Calories 130; Total Fat 1g (Saturated Fat 0g); Sodium 25mg; Total Carbohydrate 31g (Dietary Fiber 1g); Protein 0g **Exchanges:** 2 Other Carbohydrate **Carbohydrate Choices:** 2

GHOULS' BREW

For a flavor variation, use orange sherbet instead of lime, and frozen orange juice concentrate instead of limeade.

Terrifying Tip

The sherbet will float to the top, so stir the punch before pouring each serving.

Lemon-Slime Punch

PREP TIME: **15 Minutes** • START TO FINISH: **15 Minutes** • **24 servings (½ cup)**

¾ cup lemon juice

1 can (46 oz.) pineapple juice, chilled

1 pint (2 cups) lime sherbet, softened

2 bottles (20 oz each) lemon-lime carbonated beverage, chilled

1. In punch bowl, stir lemon juice, pineapple juice and sherbet until sherbet is dissolved.

2. Just before serving, slowly pour carbonated beverage into pineapple juice mixture.

1 Serving: Calories 70; Total Fat 0g (Saturated Fat 0g); Sodium 15mg; Total Carbohydrate 18g (Dietary Fiber 0g); Protein 0g **Exchanges:** ½ Fruit, ½ Other Carbohydrate **Carbohydrate Choices:** 1

Terrifying Tip

Two steps, four ingredients and 15 minutes are all you need to make this refreshing lemon and pineapple punch. For a pretty presentation, serve with lime slices.

Mud Sodas

4   cups chocolate milk, chilled

4   cups root beer, chilled

1   pint (2 cups) chocolate ice cream

1. In each of 8 tall glasses, place ½ cup milk and ½ cup root beer; stir to mix.

2. Top each serving with ¼ cup ice cream.

1 Serving: Calories 220; Total Fat 6g (Saturated Fat 4g); Sodium 120mg; Total Carbohydrate 36g (Dietary Fiber 1g); Protein 5g **Exchanges:** 2 Other Carbohydrate, ½ Low-Fat Milk; 1 Fat **Carbohydrate Choices:** 2½

Terrifying Tip

Just for fun, add swirly straws to the sodas.

Spooky Berry Shakes

PREP TIME: 15 Minutes • **START TO FINISH:** 15 Minutes • **4 shakes**

1 tablespoon white vanilla baking chips

¼ teaspoon vegetable oil

2 drops green food color

4 clear plastic cups (8- to 9-oz size)

2 cups vanilla ice cream (about 4 scoops)

1 cup frozen blueberries

1 cup frozen raspberries

2 cups milk

1. In small microwavable bowl, microwave vanilla chips and oil uncovered on High about 1 minute or until chips can be stirred smooth. Stir in green food color. With tip of knife, spread on inside of each cup to look like eyes and mouth.

2. In blender, place remaining ingredients. Cover; blend until smooth. Pour into cups. Serve immediately.

1 Shake: Calories 330; Total Fat 12g (Saturated Fat 7g); Sodium 115mg; Total Carbohydrate 48g (Dietary Fiber 5g); Protein 7g **Exchanges:** 2 Starch, 1 Other Carbohydrate, 2½ Fat **Carbohydrate Choices:** 3

Terrifying Tips

For a healthier treat, substitute yogurt for the ice cream.

Paint a spooky smile with melted white chocolate turned ghoulish green, then pour in a delicious berry blend.

S'mores Shake Shots

4 large marshmallows

1½ cups chocolate ice cream

½ cup 1% (low-fat) chocolate milk

2 graham cracker rectangles

1. Set oven control to broil. Line small cookie sheet with sides with cooking parchment paper. Place marshmallows on cookie sheet. Broil 2 minutes or until toasted.

2. Meanwhile, in blender, place ice cream, milk and 1 graham cracker. Cover; blend on medium speed until smooth.

3. Crumble remaining graham cracker; sprinkle crumbs evenly into 4 large shot glasses. Pour ice cream mixture evenly over crumbs. Top each with 1 toasted marshmallow.

1 Serving: Calories 180; Total Fat 7g (Saturated Fat 4g); Sodium 85mg; Total Carbohydrate 26g (Dietary Fiber 1g); Protein 4g **Exchanges:** 1½ Other Carbohydrate, 1½ Fat **Carbohydrate Choices:** 1½

Chilling Jack-o'-Lantern Smoothies

PREP TIME: 15 Minutes • **START TO FINISH: 15 Minutes** • **4 servings (¾ cup)**

1 tablespoon semisweet chocolate chips

4 clear plastic cups (8 to 9 oz)

3 containers (6 oz each) orange crème nonfat yogurt or harvest peach nonfat yogurt

¼ cup frozen (thawed) orange juice concentrate

1 can (11 oz) mandarin orange segments, chilled, drained

1 banana, sliced

1. In small microwavable bowl, microwave chocolate chips uncovered on High about 1 minute, stirring once, until softened and chips can be stirred smooth. With tip of knife, spread chocolate on inside of each plastic cup to look like eyes, nose and mouth of jack-o'-lantern. Refrigerate about 5 minutes or until chocolate is set.

2. Meanwhile, in blender, place remaining ingredients. Cover; blend until smooth. Pour into chocolate-painted cups. Serve immediately.

1 Serving: Calories 230; Total Fat 2g (Saturated Fat 1.5g); Sodium 65mg; Total Carbohydrate 47g (Dietary Fiber 2g); Protein 5g **Exchanges:** ½ Fruit, 2½ Other Carbohydrate, ½ Skim Milk **Carbohydrate Choices:** 3

Terrifying Tip

Kids will have fun "painting" the faces inside the cups. It works best to place the cup on its side when spreading the chocolate. Serve with a green straw to look like a pumpkin stem or garnish with a little mint leaf.

Mystifying Main Dishes

Spook your dinner guests with these ghoulish dishes.

Spiderweb Black Bean Burgers

PREP TIME: 35 Minutes • **START TO FINISH: 35 Minutes** • **6 servings (1 burger)**

- 5 teaspoons olive oil
- ¼ cup finely chopped onion
- ¼ cup finely chopped red bell pepper
- 1 clove garlic, finely chopped
- 2 cans (15 oz each) black beans, drained, rinsed
- 3 tablespoons unseasoned dry bread crumbs
- ¼ cup chopped fresh cilantro
- 1 teaspoon finely chopped chipotle chiles in adobo sauce (from 7-oz can)
- ½ teaspoon ground cumin
- 1 egg
- ½ cup sour cream
- 1½ teaspoons adobo sauce (from can of chipotle chiles)
- 6 hamburger buns, split 6 leaves lettuce
- 6 slices tomato

1. In 12-inch nonstick skillet, heat 1 teaspoon of the oil over medium-high heat. Cook onion, bell pepper and garlic in oil 2 minutes, stirring frequently, until tender.

2. In large bowl, slightly mash black beans. Add onion mixture, bread crumbs, cilantro, chipotle chiles, cumin and egg; mix until blended. Shape mixture into 6 patties, about ½ inch thick.

3. In same skillet, heat 2 teaspoons oil over medium heat. Cook 3 patties in oil 2 to 3 minutes on each side or until browned. Remove from skillet; cover to keep warm. Repeat with 2 teaspoons oil and remaining 3 patties.

4. In small bowl, mix sour cream and adobo sauce until blended. Spoon mixture into small resealable food-storage plastic bag; seal bag. Cut off tiny corner of bag.

5. On bun bottoms, place lettuce, tomato and patties. Squeeze bag to pipe sour cream mixture in spiral pattern on patty, starting from center. Pipe rays outward from center to make web design. Serve with bun tops.

1 Serving: Calories 277; Total Fat 11g (Saturated Fat 4g); Sodium 450mg; Total Carbohydrate 38g (Dietary Fiber 9g); Protein 12g **Exchanges:** 2½ Starch, 1 Very Lean Meat, 1½ Fat **Carbohydrate Choices:** 2½

Chicken Enchilada Mummies

PREP TIME: 30 Minutes • **START TO FINISH: 1 Hour 20 Minutes** • **12 enchiladas**

 2   teaspoons vegetable oil

 6   boneless, skinless chicken breasts (about 2½ lb), cut into 1-inch pieces

 1   medium onion, chopped (½ cup)

 1   teaspoon ground cumin

 1   teaspoon garlic salt

 ½   teaspoon dried oregano leaves

1½   cups sour cream

 ¾   cup chopped roasted red bell peppers (from a jar)

 1   can (4.5 oz) chopped green chiles

 3   cups finely shredded Mexican cheese blend (12 oz)

12   flour tortillas (8 inch)

 2   cans (10 oz each) enchilada sauce

1. Heat oven to 350°F. Spray 13x9-inch (3-quart) and 8x8-inch (2-quart) baking dishes with cooking spray.

2. In 12-inch skillet, heat oil over medium-high heat. Add chicken and onion; cook and stir 4 to 5 minutes or until chicken is no longer pink in center. Stir in cumin, garlic salt and oregano. Cook 1 minute longer; drain if necessary. Pour chicken mixture into large bowl.

3. Reserve 2 tablespoons sour cream in small bowl; refrigerate. Into bowl of chicken mixture, stir remaining sour cream, roasted peppers, chiles and 1½ cups of the cheese blend.

4. Spread heaping ¾ cup chicken mixture in center of each tortilla. Roll up tortillas; arrange 8 seam-side down in 13x9-inch baking dish and 4 seam-side down in 8x8-inch baking dish.

5. Top each baking dish evenly with enchilada sauce. Sprinkle with remaining 1½ cups cheese. Spray 2 sheets of foil with cooking spray; cover each baking dish with foil, sprayed side down.

6. Bake about 50 minutes or until enchiladas are hot. Place reserved 2 tablespoons sour cream into resealable plastic food-storage snack bag. Seal bag; cut off 1 corner of bag. Squeeze bag to pipe eyes and mouth on each mummy.

1 Enchilada: Calories 390; Total Fat 21g (Saturated Fat 10g); Sodium 880mg; Total Carbohydrate 19g (Dietary Fiber 1g); Protein 30g **Exchanges:** 1 Starch, 4 Very Lean Meat, 3½ Fat **Carbohydrate Choices:** 1

Taco Monster Mouths

PREP TIME: 30 Minutes • **START TO FINISH:** 30 Minutes • 6 servings (1 taco each)

2 plum (Roma) tomatoes, cut length-wise into 3 pieces

12 large pimiento-stuffed green olives

3 slices (½ oz each) American cheese

6 taco shells that stand on their own (from 4.7 oz box)

½ lb lean (at least 80%) ground beef

2 tablespoons 40% less-sodium taco seasoning mix

⅓ cup water

Shredded lettuce, if desired

1. Cut each tomato lengthwise into 3 pieces. Remaining inside of tomato may be chopped for additional taco filling, if desired.

2. Cut slit into 1 side of each olive to make a flat side. Cut each of the slices of cheese in half vertically in a zigzag line to look like teeth.

3. Heat oven to 350°F. Arrange taco shells on ungreased cookie sheet. Bake 5 to 7 minutes or until hot. Meanwhile, in 10-inch skillet, cook ground beef over medium-high heat 5 to 7 minutes, stirring frequently, until thoroughly cooked; drain. Stir in taco seasoning mix and water. Reduce heat to medium; cook about 5 minutes, stirring frequently until water has evaporated.

4. To assemble, fill tacos with desired fillings so that beef is on the top. Placing each taco on its side on serving plate, insert 1 tomato slice into meat filling to look like tongue. Place 1 cheese slice with zigzag edge toward meat along top side of taco between the shell and the filling. Place 2 olives, flat sides down, to look like eyes on top of shell.

1 Serving: Calories 180 ; Total Fat 11g (Saturated Fat 3.5g); Sodium 490mg; Total Carbohydrate 12g (Dietary Fiber 1g); Protein 9g **Exchanges:** 1 Starch, 1 High-Fat Meat **Carbohydrate Choices:** 1

Terrifying Tips

Ground turkey can be used in place of the ground beef.

Sneaky Snake Pinwheels

PREP TIME: 20 Minutes • **START TO FINISH: 1 Hour 20 Minutes** • **About 16 servings**

2   squares (7¼x8¾ inch) flatbread (from 8-oz package)

1   package (3 oz) fat-free cream cheese, softened

    Half a medium red bell pepper, chopped (about ¼ cup)

4   leaves romaine lettuce

12   thin slices hard salami (about 2½ oz)

    Half a large pickle, cut lengthwise into 4 spears (from 32-oz jar kosher dill pickle halves)

2   small red bell pepper pieces, cut into snakelike tongues

1. Spread each flatbread with half of the cream cheese to within 1 inch from edge of bread. Sprinkle each with 2 tablespoons chopped bell pepper.

2. Top each with 2 leaves romaine lettuce and 6 thin salami slices, leaving 1-inch border on both long sides of each. Place 2 pickle slices end to end lengthwise on each flatbread. Tightly roll up flatbread.

3. Wrap flatbread rolls individually in plastic wrap. Refrigerate at least 1 hour but no longer than 24 hours. With serrated knife, cut into 1-inch slices; secure each slice with toothpick. Arrange on large platter in twisty snakelike shape. Arrange front piece at angle slightly away from the body to look like head, place 1 red pepper piece on underside of pinwheel to look like tongue. Arrange rear piece at angle for end of snake.

1 Serving: Calories 40; Total Fat 1.5g (Saturated Fat 0g); Sodium 190mg; Total Carbohydrate 4g (Dietary Fiber 1g); Protein 3g **Exchanges:** ½ Starch **Carbohydrate Choices:** 0

Terrifying Tip

Look for flatbread in the deli department of your local grocery store. If you can't find it, use 8-inch round tortillas.

Serpent Subs

PREP TIME: 20 Minutes • START TO FINISH: 1 Hour 10 Minutes • 24 servings (1 slice)

4 cans Pillsbury® refrigerated crusty French loaf

½ cup olive oil and vinegar dressing

1 lb thinly sliced cooked ham

48 thin slices hard salami (about 18 oz)

1 lb provolone cheese, thinly sliced

1 cup sliced pepperoncini peppers (bottled Italian peppers), drained

1 cup mixed sliced pitted green and ripe olives

1 cup chopped drained roasted red bell peppers (from 7-oz jar)

12 leaves leaf lettuce

4 pitted large green or ripe olives

1 large piece roasted red bell pepper (from 7-oz jar)

1. Heat oven to 350°F. Grease 2 large cookie sheets. Place 2 loaves of dough, seam side down, on each cookie sheet; form dough into continuous S shape. With kitchen scissors, cut diagonal slits across tops of loaves as directed on can. Bake 26 to 30 minutes or until golden brown. Cool 20 minutes.

2. Cut each loaf in half horizontally. Drizzle cut sides with dressing. On bottoms of loaves, evenly layer ham, salami, cheese, pepperoncini peppers, sliced olives, chopped roasted peppers and lettuce. Cover with tops of loaves. Arrange sandwiches in S shape on large platter or cutting board.

3. Add large olives for eyes; secure with toothpicks. Cut roasted pepper piece in half to look like tongue and insert 1 piece into end of each sandwich. To serve, cut crosswise into 2-inch slices.

1 Serving: Calories 310; Total Fat 14g (Saturated Fat 6g); Sodium 1210mg; Total Carbohydrate 27g (Dietary Fiber 1g); Protein 18g **Exchanges:** 2 Starch, 2 Medium-Fat Meat, ½ Fat **Carbohydrate Choices:** 2

Terrifying Tip

Try alternative fillings such as pesto and your favorite sliced deli meats and cheeses.

Grilled Ham and Cheese Boo Bites

PREP TIME: 20 Minutes • **START TO FINISH: 20 Minutes** • **4 sandwiches**

8 slices whole wheat bread

¼ cup chives-and-onion cream cheese spread (from 8-oz container)

8 slices deli ham

4 slices sharp Cheddar cheese

2 tablespoons butter or margarine

1. Using paring knife, cut out eyes, nose and mouth to look like pumpkin face in each of 4 slices of the bread; set aside. On remaining 4 slices bread, spread 1 tablespoon of the cream cheese, and top with 2 slices ham and 1 slice cheese. Top each with cut bread slice.

2. In 12-inch nonstick skillet, melt 1 tablespoon of the butter over medium-high heat. Place 2 sandwiches face down in skillet; cook 1 to 2 minutes or until face is light brown and cheese is beginning to melt. Turn sandwich, reduce heat to medium-low; cook 3 to 4 minutes longer or until light brown and cheese is melted. Repeat with remaining 1 tablespoon butter and 2 sandwiches. Serve immediately.

1 Sandwich: Calories 380; Total Fat 21g (Saturated Fat 12g); Sodium 1050mg; Total Carbohydrate 25g (Dietary Fiber 4g); Protein 22g **Exchanges:** 1½ Starch, 2½ High-Fat Meat **Carbohydrate Choices:** 1½

Terrifying Tips

If you have alphabet cookie cutters, cut "BOO" out of 4 slices of bread and cut each sandwich into thirds.

Use an electric or stovetop griddle, and cook sandwiches all at one time.

RIP Banana PB 'n J Sandwiches

PREP TIME: 30 Minutes • **START TO FINISH: 30 Minutes** • **8 servings (1 sandwich)**

16 slices bread

8 tablespoons creamy peanut butter

¼ cup grape jelly

1 small banana, cut into 24 slices

1. Place 1 bread slice on top of another. Cut 4x2 ½-inch "casket" shape from longest part of bread slices. Cut ½ inch off both top corners of bread slices. Repeat with remaining bread slices.

2. Separate bread slices. On each bottom slice, spread 1 tablespoon peanut butter. Top with 1 teaspoon jelly and 3 banana slices. Replace top slices of bread.

3. Place remaining 1 tablespoon jelly in small resealable food-storage plastic bag; seal bag. Cut off tiny corner of bag. Squeeze bag to pipe RIP (Rest In Peace) on each "casket" sandwich. Serve, or cover and refrigerate.

1 Serving: Calories 280; Total Fat 11g (Saturated Fat 2g); Sodium 430mg; Total Carbohydrate 37g (Dietary Fiber 2g); Protein 9g **Exchanges:** 2 Starch, ½ Other Carbohydrate, ½ High-Fat Meat, 1 Fat **Carbohydrate Choices:** 2½

Terrifying Tip

Feel free to use a spreadable fruit or other jam or preserves in place of the jelly. Flavored peanut butter is also a tasty filling for these "coffin-wiches."

Spooky Spiderweb Pizza

PREP TIME: 15 Minutes • **START TO FINISH: 35 Minutes** • **12 servings**

1 can Pillsbury® refrigerated classic pizza crust

28 slices pepperoni (half of 3.5-oz package)

¼ cup sliced ripe olives

1 cup shredded mozzarella cheese (4 oz)

1 can (8 oz) pizza sauce

¼ cup refrigerated garlic Alfredo pasta sauce (from 10-oz container)

1. Heat oven to 400°F. Spray 14-inch round pizza pan with cooking spray. Unroll dough on pan; shape into round to desired thickness. Bake 8 minutes. Arrange pepperoni and 3 tablespoons of the olives on crust to within 1 inch of edge. Sprinkle with cheese. Evenly pour pizza sauce over toppings; gently spreading to cover.

2. In small resealable food-storage plastic bag, place Alfredo sauce; seal bag. Cut off tiny corner of bag. Squeeze bag to drizzle Alfredo sauce in circles over pizza sauce, starting from outer edge continuously to center. Pull knife through Alfredo sauce, starting from center to outside edge, changing direction with every pull, to look like spiderweb. Sprinkle remaining 1 tablespoon olives on top to look like spiders. Bake 8 to 12 minutes longer or until crust is golden brown. Cut into wedges to serve.

1 Serving: Calories 230; Total Fat 12g (Saturated Fat 6g); Sodium 640mg; Total Carbohydrate 19g (Dietary Fiber 0g); Protein 10g **Exchanges:** 1 Starch, ½ Other Carbohydrate, 1 High-Fat Meat, ½ Fat **Carbohydrate Choices:** 1

Terrifying Tip

The remaining Alfredo sauce can be frozen until needed for another use, such as tossing with hot linguine.

Bewitched Double-Crust Cheese Pizza

PREP TIME: 15 Minutes • **START TO FINISH: 30 Minutes** • **8 servings**

3 cups Original Bisquick® mix

⅔ cup very hot water

1 can (8 oz) pizza sauce

2 cups shredded Mexican cheese blend (8 oz)

½ teaspoon spicy pizza seasoning

1. Move oven rack to lowest position. Heat oven to 450°F. Spray 12-inch pizza pan with cooking spray.

2. In large bowl, stir Bisquick mix and hot water with fork until soft dough forms; beat vigorously 20 strokes. Divide dough in half. Press half of the dough in pizza pan, using fingers dipped in Bisquick mix; pinch edge to form ½-inch rim. Spread pizza sauce over dough. In medium bowl, mix cheese and pizza seasoning; sprinkle over pizza sauce.

3. Place remaining dough on surface dusted with Bisquick mix; roll in Bisquick mix to coat. Shape into a ball; knead 5 times. Roll dough into 14-inch circle. Use cookie cutters in Halloween shapes to cut shapes from dough (leave 1 inch of dough between cutouts and leave 1 inch of edge of dough uncut). Fold dough circle in half; place over pizza and unfold. Seal edges. Place dough cutouts on top of pizza, if desired.

4. Bake 12 to 15 minutes or until crust is golden brown and cheese is melted.

1 Serving: Calories 300; Total Fat 14g (Saturated Fat 7g); Sodium 850mg; Total Carbohydrate 32g (Dietary Fiber 1g); Protein 10g **Exchanges:** 1½ Starch, ½ Other Carbohydrate, 1 High-Fat Meat, 1 Fat **Carbohydrate Choices:** 2

Terrifying Tips

If you prefer, or if you can't find the Mexican cheese blend, make your own blend. Mix ½ cup each shredded mozzarella, shredded provolone, shredded Cheddar and grated Parmesan cheeses.

Smaller Halloween cutouts will allow you to have a few more designs and make it easier to transfer the cutouts to the pizza.

Pizza Pot Pies

PREP TIME: 20 Minutes • **START TO FINISH: 40 Minutes** • **4 servings**

1 lb lean (at least 80%) ground beef

1 medium onion, chopped (½ cup)

1 small green bell pepper, chopped (½ cup)

1 can (8 oz) pizza sauce

1 can (4 oz) mushroom stems and pieces, drained

1 cup shredded mozzarella cheese (4 oz)

1 cup Original Bisquick® mix

¼ cup boiling water

1. Heat oven to 375°F. Grease four 10- to 12-ounce casseroles. In 10-inch skillet, cook beef, onion and bell pepper over medium heat, stirring occasionally, until beef is brown; drain.

2. Stir pizza sauce and mushrooms into beef. Heat to boiling; reduce heat. Simmer uncovered 5 minutes, stirring occasionally. Spoon beef mixture into casseroles. Sprinkle ¼ cup of the cheese on each.

3. In small bowl, stir Bisquick mix and boiling water until soft dough forms; beat vigorously 20 strokes. Turn dough onto surface dusted with baking mix; gently roll in baking mix to coat. Shape into ball; knead about 10 times or until smooth. Divide dough into 4 balls. Pat each ball into circle the size of diameter of casserole. Place each circle on beef mixture in casserole.

4. Bake 15 to 20 minutes or until crust is very light brown.

1 Serving: Calories 605; Total Fat 40g (Saturated Fat 15g); Sodium 1990mg; Total Carbohydrate 29g (Dietary Fiber 2g); Protein 34g **Exchanges:** 1½ Starch, 1 Vegetable, 4 Medium-Fat Meat, 1 Fat **Carbohydrate Choices:** 2

Terrifying Tips

For variety, add sliced olives, chopped tomatoes or sliced pepperoni, cut into fourths, to the pizza sauce mixture.

For a special Halloween treat, use a small cookie cutter to cut a jack-o'-lantern, cat, pumpkin or moon shape out of the dough circle before putting it on the beef mixture.

Spiderweb Pot Pies

PREP TIME: 25 Minutes • **START TO FINISH:** 45 Minutes • 6 servings

3 cans (8 oz each) Pillsbury® Crescent Recipe Creations® refrigerated seamless dough sheet

2 cups shredded deli rotisserie chicken (from 2-lb chicken)

1 cup frozen baby sweet peas (from 12-oz bag), thawed

1 cup frozen corn (from 12-oz bag), thawed

½ cup milk

2 cans (10¾ oz each) condensed cream of potato soup

1 cup shredded Cheddar cheese (4 oz)

½ cup sour cream

12 pitted large ripe olives

1. Heat oven to 350°F. Line 3 cookie sheets with cooking parchment paper. Unroll 1 dough sheet on work surface. Cut dough in half; cut each half into 9 strips. Place strips on 1 cookie sheet; refrigerate until ready to use.

2. Unroll remaining dough sheets. Place 4½-inch round biscuit cutter on dough; place 3½-inch round biscuit cutter inside larger cutter. Cut out thin 4½-inch ring of dough between cutters. Repeat process, making a total of 6 large dough rings. Place on cookie sheet; refrigerate. Place 2½-inch round biscuit cutter on dough; place 1½-inch round biscuit cutter inside larger cutter. Cut out thin 2½-inch ring of dough between cutters. Repeat process, making a total of 6 medium dough rings.

3. Place 1½-inch round cutter on dough; place 1-inch round cutter inside larger cutter. Cut out thin 1½-inch ring of dough between cutters. Repeat process, making a total of 6 small dough rings. Cut out 6 tiny circles from remaining dough. In 3-quart saucepan, mix chicken, peas, corn, milk and soup. Cook over medium heat until bubbly; stir in cheese and sour cream. Spoon ¾ cup hot chicken mixture into each of 6 (1-cup) individual baking dishes. Place cups at least 4 inches apart on 2 cookie sheets.

4. Place 3 dough strips crisscrossing over rim of each pot pie to look like spider legs. Onto each pot pie, place large, medium and small dough rings. Place tiny dough circle in center of each. Bake 20 minutes or until crust is golden brown. Cut each olive in half; set aside 6 olive halves for spider bodies. Cut remaining olive pieces into 48 small pieces for spider legs. Arrange olive half and 8 pieces on each pot pie.

1 Serving: Calories 771; Total Fat 39g (Saturated Fat 16g); Sodium 1823mg; Total Carbohydrate 67g (Dietary Fiber 3g); Protein 32g **Exchanges:** 4½ Starch, 2 Very Lean Meat, 1 High-Fat Meat, 5 Fat **Carbohydrate Choices:** 4½

Scary Slow-Cooked Chili

PREP TIME: 20 Minutes • **START TO FINISH:** 7 Hours 20 Minutes • 6 servings (1½ cups each)

1   lb lean (at least 80%) ground beef

½   lb bulk Italian pork sausage

1   medium onion, chopped (about ½ cup)

1   can (28 oz) whole tomatoes, undrained, cut up

1   can (15 oz) tomato sauce

2   teaspoons chili powder

1   to 1½ teaspoons ground cumin

1   teaspoon sugar

1   teaspoon dried oregano leaves

1   can (15 oz) spicy chili beans in sauce

1   can (15 oz) chick peas (garbanzo beans), drained, rinsed

6   slices (1 oz each) American cheese

1. In 10-inch skillet, cook beef, sausage and onion over medium-high heat 5 to 7 minutes, stirring frequently, until beef is thoroughly cooked and sausage is no longer pink; drain.

2. In 3½- to 4-quart slow cooker, mix beef mixture and all remaining ingredients except cheese.

3. Cover; cook on Low heat setting 7 to 8 hours. Use a Halloween-themed cookie cutter to cut out shape from cheese. Top individual servings with cut outs.

1 Serving: Calories 420; Total Fat 16g (Saturated Fat 5g); Sodium 1260mg; Total Carbohydrate 41g (Dietary Fiber 10g); Protein 28g **Exchanges:** 1½ Starch, 1 Other Carbohydrate, 1 Vegetable, 3 Medium-Fat Meat **Carbohydrate Choices:** 3

Spooky Shepherd's Pie

PREP TIME: 30 Minutes • **START TO FINISH: 55 Minutes** • **6 servings**

1 lb lean (at least 80%) ground beef

1 medium onion, coarsely chopped (½ cup)

2½ cups frozen mixed vegetables (from 12-oz bag)

1 can (14.5 oz) diced tomatoes with Italian herbs, undrained

1 jar (12 oz) beef gravy

1¾ cups water

2 tablespoons butter or margarine

¼ teaspoon garlic powder

½ cup milk

2¼ cups plain mashed potato mix (dry)

¼ cup grated Parmesan cheese

1 egg, slightly beaten

1. Heat oven to 375°F. Spray 12-inch skillet with cooking spray. Cook beef and onion in skillet over medium-high heat 5 to 7 minutes, stirring frequently, until beef is thoroughly cooked; drain.

2. Set aside 12 peas for garnish. Add remaining frozen vegetables, tomatoes and gravy to beef. Heat to boiling. Reduce heat to medium-low; cover and cook 8 to 10 minutes, stirring occasionally, until vegetables are crisp-tender.

3. Meanwhile, in 2-quart saucepan, heat water, butter and garlic powder to boiling. Remove from heat; stir in milk, dry potato mix and cheese. Stir in egg until well blended.

4. Spoon beef mixture into ungreased 8-inch square (2-quart) or oval (2½-quart) glass baking dish. With large spoon, make 6 mounds of potato mixture on top of beef mixture to look like ghosts. Place 2 reserved peas on each mound to look like eyes.

5. Bake 20 to 25 minutes or until potatoes are set and mixture is hot.

1 Serving: Calories 590; Total Fat 17g (Saturated Fat 8g); Sodium 630mg; Total Carbohydrate 82g (Dietary Fiber 10g); Protein 28g **Exchanges:** 4 Starch, 1 Other Carbohydrate, 1 Vegetable, 2 Medium-Fat Meat, 1 Fat **Carbohydrate Choices:** 5½

Terrifying Tip

Use kitchen scissors to cut the tomatoes. Cut them just after adding them to the slow cooker while they're still on top and easy to reach.

Bloody Barbecue Ribs

PREP TIME: 30 Minutes • **START TO FINISH: 3 Hours 5 Minutes** • **8 servings (3 ribs)**

Ribs

4   lb pork baby back ribs

4   teaspoons Montreal steak grill seasoning

Barbecue Sauce

1   teaspoon vegetable oil

¾   cup chopped onion

4   cups ketchup

3   chipotle chiles in adobo sauce (from 7-oz can), finely chopped

¼   cup molasses

¼   cup cider vinegar

2   tablespoons packed dark brown sugar

½   teaspoon garlic powder

½   teaspoon Dijon mustard

1. Heat oven to 300°F. Place ribs in ungreased 15x10x1-inch pan. Sprinkle grill seasoning all over ribs. Cover with foil. Bake 3 hours.

2. Meanwhile, in 3-quart saucepan, heat oil over medium heat. Cook onion in oil, stirring occasionally, until tender. Add remaining sauce ingredients. Heat to simmering; simmer uncovered 15 minutes, stirring occasionally. Remove from heat. Cool completely.

3. Set oven control to broil. Brush ribs with 1½ cups of the barbecue sauce. Broil with tops about 3 inches from heat 4 minutes or until sauce begins to caramelize on ribs. Serve ribs with additional sauce. Refrigerate any remaining sauce.

1 Serving: Calories 816; Total Fat 55g (Saturated Fat 20g); Sodium 1938mg; Total Carbohydrate 43g (Dietary Fiber 1g); Protein 39g **Exchanges:** 3 Other Carbohydrate, 5 High-Fat Meat, 3 Fat **Carbohydrate Choices:** 3

Skewered Worms

PREP TIME: 20 Minutes • **START TO FINISH: 2 Hours 15 Minutes** • **8 servings**

Beef

16	wooden skewers
⅔	cup olive oil
1	tablespoon grated lemon peel
⅓	cup lemon juice
1	tablespoon chopped fresh thyme leaves
¾	teaspoon salt
3	cloves garlic, finely chopped
2	lb beef flank steak

Spicy Sauce

1	cup ketchup
2	cloves garlic, peeled
1	canned chipotle chile in adobo sauce

1. In 11x8-inch baking dish, soak skewers in water at least 30 minutes.

2. Meanwhile, in 1-gallon resealable food-storage plastic bag, mix oil, lemon peel, lemon juice, thyme leaves, salt and garlic. Slice beef across the grain into ¼-inch strips. Place beef in oil mixture. Seal bag; refrigerate 2 to 4 hours to marinate.

3. Meanwhile, in blender or food processor, place sauce ingredients. Cover; blend on high speed until smooth.

4. Thread beef on skewers, twirling 2 to 3 beef strips around each skewer to look like worms. Reserve any remaining marinade.

5. Set oven control to broil. Place skewers on broiler pan. Broil with tops 4 to 6 inches from heat 3 minutes. Turn skewers, and brush with marinade. (Discard any remaining marinade.) Broil 2 to 3 minutes longer or until desired doneness. Serve with sauce.

1 Serving: Calories 380; Total Fat 23g (Saturated Fat 4g); Sodium 630mg; Total Carbohydrate 9g (Dietary Fiber 0g); Protein 34g **Exchanges:** ½ Other Carbohydrate, 5 Lean Meat, 1½ Fat **Carbohydrate Choices:** ½

Terrifying Tip

For easier slicing, place steak in freezer for 1 hour or until firm but not frozen; slice thinly across grain of meat.

Scary Pancakes

PREP TIME: 30 Minutes   •   **START TO FINISH:** 30 Minutes

• **8 servings (1 pancake and 2 tablespoons topping each)**

1   container (6 oz) orange crème lowfat yogurt

¼   cup maple-flavored syrup

2   cups Original Bisquick® mix

1¼   cups milk

1   egg

1   teaspoon unsweetened baking cocoa

1   teaspoon sugar

Terrifying Tip

Any flavor of yogurt can be substituted for the orange flavor.

1. In small bowl, mix yogurt and maple syrup until well blended. Set aside.

2. In medium bowl, mix baking mix, milk and egg until well blended. In small bowl, mix 2 tablespoons of the batter, the cocoa and sugar until well blended.

3. Heat large nonstick electric griddle or 12-inch nonstick skillet to 375°F. Oil hot griddle.

4. For each pancake, drop three ¼- to ½-inch drops of dark batter about 1 to 1½ inches apart forming eyes and mouth of ghost. Cook about 30 seconds. Immediately pour ¼ cup regular batter; start the pour to cover the "eyes and mouth" and continue the pour downward to form an irregular ghostly shape. Cook 1 to 2 minutes or until pancake is puffed and dry around edges. Turn pancake; cook about 1 minute longer or until other side is golden brown. Serve with syrup mixture.

1 Serving: Calories 200; Total Fat 6g (Saturated Fat 2g); Sodium 470mg; Total Carbohydrate 33g (Dietary Fiber 0g); Protein 5g **Exchanges:** 1 Starch, 1½ Other Carbohydrate, 1 Fat **Carbohydrate Choices:** 2

Great Pumpkin Chocolate Chip Pancakes

PREP TIME: 20 Minutes • **START TO FINISH: 20 Minutes**

• **10 servings (1 pancake and 1½ tablespoons syrup)**

Orange Syrup

- ⅔ **cup real maple syrup**
- ⅓ **cup light corn syrup**
- 2 **tablespoons butter**
- ⅛ **teaspoon orange gel food color**

Pancakes

- 1 **cup half-and-half**
- 2 **tablespoons lemon juice**
- 2 **cups Original Bisquick® mix**
- 1 **tablespoon sugar**
- 2 **teaspoons baking powder**
- 2 **eggs, separated**
- 1 **teaspoon vanilla**
- 1 **cup semisweet chocolate chips (6 oz)**

1. In 1-quart saucepan, heat maple syrup, corn syrup and butter over medium-low heat until butter is melted. Remove from heat; stir in food color. Set aside.

2. In large bowl, stir together half-and-half and lemon juice; let stand 2 minutes. Stir in Bisquick mix, sugar, baking powder, egg yolks and vanilla with wire whisk or fork until blended. Stir in chocolate chips. In small bowl, beat egg whites with electric mixer on high speed until soft peaks form. Fold beaten egg whites into batter.

3. Heat griddle to 350°F or heat 12-inch nonstick skillet over medium heat. Grease with melted butter. Place pumpkin pancake mold onto griddle with handle up; heat until hot.

4. For each pancake, pour ⅓ cup batter into mold on hot griddle. Cook until bubbles break on surface and edges just begin to dry. Remove mold. Turn; cook about 1 minute or until golden brown. Serve with orange syrup.

1 Serving: Calories 340; Total Fat 14.5g (Saturated Fat 7g); Sodium 463mg; Total Carbohydrate 51g (Dietary Fiber 1g); Protein 5g **Exchanges:** 1 Starch, 2½ Other Carbohydrate, 3 Fat **Carbohydrate Choices:** 3½

Cyclops Eyeballs

PREP TIME: 10 Minutes • **START TO FINISH: 30 Minutes** • **8 servings**

1 can Pillsbury® Grands!® Homestyle refrigerated buttermilk biscuits

8 eggs

1 tablespoon ketchup

1. Heat oven to 375°F. Separate dough into 8 biscuits. Lightly grease 8 (6-oz) custard cups with shortening, or spray with cooking spray. Press each biscuit in bottom and up side of each custard cup, rolling edges to form rim. Break 1 egg into each cup. Place cups on large cookie sheet with sides.

2. Bake 18 to 22 minutes or until biscuit is golden brown and egg is cooked through. Spoon ketchup into small resealable food-storage plastic bag. Cut small hole in 1 corner of bag. Squeeze ketchup onto each egg to make it look like bloodshot eye. Serve warm.

1 Serving: Calories 260; Total Fat 13g (Saturated Fat 4.5g); Sodium 680mg; Total Carbohydrate 25g (Dietary Fiber 0g); Protein 10g **Exchanges:** 1½ Starch, 1 Medium-Fat Meat, 1½ Fat **Carbohydrate Choices:** 1½

Terrifying Tips

Serve with ham, Canadian bacon or breakfast sausage.

Strips of tomato can be used to form the bloodshot eye instead of the ketchup.

Spooky Cupcakes & Cakes

Halloween is all about scaring up some fun—and these are frightfully delightful!

Boneyard Dirt Pops

1   **package (16.6 oz) creme-filled chocolate sandwich cookies**

1   **package (8 oz) cream cheese, softened**

1   **bag (14 oz) dark cocoa candy melts**

16   **paper lollipop sticks**

     Bone-shaped candy sprinkles

1   **block white polystyrene foam**

1. Line 2 cookie sheets with waxed paper. In food processor, place cookies. Cover; process using quick on-and-off motions, until consistency of fine crumbs. Reserve ¼ cup of the crumbs. In large bowl, mix remaining crumbs and the cream cheese until well blended. Roll into 1½-inch balls. Place on cookie sheets. Freeze 30 minutes or until firm.

2. In small microwavable bowl, microwave half of the candy melts on High 1 minute 30 seconds, then in 15-second intervals, until melted; stir until smooth.

3. Move cake balls from freezer to refrigerator. Remove several cake balls from refrigerator at a time. Dip tip of 1 lollipop stick about ½ inch into melted candy and insert stick into 1 cake ball no more than halfway. Dip pop into melted candy to cover; tap off excess. Immediately sprinkle with reserved crumbs and candy sprinkles. Poke opposite end of stick into foam block. Repeat with remaining candy melts, cake balls, crumbs and candy sprinkles.

1 Serving: Calories 308; Total Fat 17g (Saturated Fat 10g); Sodium 215mg; Total Carbohydrate 38.5g (Dietary Fiber 1g); Protein 2g **Exchanges:** 2½ Other Carbohydrate, 3½ Fat **Carbohydrate Choices:** 2½

Terrifying Tip

Add gummy worm candies to tops of dirt pops, if desired.

Witchy Cake Balls

PREP TIME: 1 Hour • **START TO FINISH: 1 Hour 40 Minutes** • **12 servings (1 witchy ball)**

Cake

1 box chocolate fudge cake mix with pudding in the mix

Water, vegetable oil and eggs called for on cake mix box

Frosting and Decorations

1 container (1 lb) chocolate creamy ready-to-spread frosting

8 oz dark cocoa candy melts or coating wafers

12 sugar-style ice cream cones with pointed ends

Assorted Halloween candy sprinkles or nonpareils

12 thin chocolate wafer cookies

1 bag (16 oz) green or dark green candy melts

1 tube (4.25 oz) green decorating icing

4 pull-apart black or red licorice twists, separated, cut into 2½-inch pieces

24 candy-coated chocolate candies

12 pieces candy corn

1. Heat oven to 350°F. Grease bottom only of 13x9-inch pan with shortening or cooking spray. Make and bake cake mix as directed on box for 13x9-inch pan, using water, oil and eggs. Cool 10 minutes; remove cake from pan to cooling rack. Cool 15 minutes.

2. Line cookie sheet with waxed paper. In large bowl, crumble cake. Add chocolate frosting; mix well with back of spoon. Use ice cream scoop to scoop cake mixture into 2½-inch balls onto cookie sheet. Freeze about 15 minutes or until firm. Refrigerate to keep chilled.

3. In medium microwavable bowl, microwave dark cocoa candy melts uncovered on Medium (50%) 1 minute, then in 15-second increments, until melted; stir until smooth. Using small food-safe brush, brush melted chocolate coating over each ice cream cone to coat completely; decorate as desired with sprinkles before coating hardens. Dip open end of each ice cream cone into remaining melted chocolate coating; place dipped end of each cone onto a chocolate wafer cookie, pressing lightly, to form hat and brim. Let stand until set.

4. In medium microwavable bowl, microwave green candy melts uncovered on Medium (50%) 1 minute, then in 15-second increments, until melted; stir until smooth. Place 1 cake ball on a fork; dip cake ball into melted green coating to cover. Gently tap off any excess coating. Place coated ball on cookie sheet; top with 1 chocolate-coated cone hat, pressing gently. Repeat with remaining cake balls and cone hats. Let stand until set. Squeeze icing from tube onto bottom edge of each chocolate wafer cookie; attach licorice pieces with icing to form hair. Use icing to attach 2 chocolate candies for eyes and 1 piece candy corn for nose.

1 Serving: Calories 792; Total Fat 35g (Saturated Fat 17g); Sodium 546mg; Total Carbohydrate 115g (Dietary Fiber 3g); Protein 6g **Exchanges:** 2 Starch, 5½ Other Carbohydrate, 7 Fat **Carbohydrate Choices:** 7½

Tarantula Treats

PREP TIME: 1 Hour 30 Minutes • **START TO FINISH: 2 Hours** • **48 servings (1 treat)**

Cake

1 **box dark chocolate cake mix with pudding**

Water, vegetable oil and eggs called for on cake mix box

Frosting and Decorations

1 **bag (12 oz) semisweet chocolate chips (2 cups)**

2 **tablespoons butter (do not use margarine)**

¾ **cup whipping cream**

2 **tablespoons light corn syrup**

96 **orange jelly beans, if desired**

Black string licorice, cut into 1-inch pieces, if desired

Chocolate sprinkles, if desired

1. Heat oven to 350°F. Place mini paper baking cup in each of 48 mini muffin cups. Make and bake cupcakes as directed on box for miniature-size cupcakes, using water, oil and eggs. Remove from pans to cooling racks. Cool completely, about 20 minutes.

2. Meanwhile, in medium bowl, place chocolate chips and butter. In 1-quart saucepan, heat whipping cream and corn syrup to boiling; remove from heat. Pour over chocolate chips and butter; let stand 1 minute. Stir with wire whisk until smooth. Cover; refrigerate until spreadable, about 30 minutes, stirring occasionally.

3. Frost cupcakes with frosting. Place 2 jelly beans on each cupcake for eyes. Press 8 licorice pieces into frosting on each cupcake for legs. Decorate with chocolate sprinkles.

1 Serving: Calories 123; Total Fat 6g (Saturated Fat 3g); Sodium 104mg; Total Carbohydrate 16g (Dietary Fiber 1g); Protein 1g **Exchanges:** 1 Other Carbohydrate, 1 Fat **Carbohydrate Choices:** 1

Terrifying Tip

If you don't have time to make 48 miniature treats, tarantulas can easily be made using regular-size muffin cups. Simply follow the instructions on the cake mix package for regular-size cupcakes. Be sure to cut the licorice into 2-inch pieces instead of 1-inch pieces for the legs.

Awesome Alien Cupcakes

PREP TIME: 55 Minutes • **START TO FINISH: 1 Hour 55 Minutes** • **24 servings (1 cupcake)**

Cake

1 box devil's food cake mix with pudding in the mix

Water, vegetable oil and eggs called for on cake mix box

Frosting and Decorations

6 cups Kix® cereal

3 tablespoons butter

4 cups miniature marshmallows

¼ teaspoon orange neon gel or paste food color (from 2.7-oz tube)

48 gummy peach ring candies

48 candy-coated chocolate candies

Black decorating gel

48 thin pretzel sticks (2¼ inch)

20 drops green food color

1 container (12 oz) fluffy white whipped ready-to-spread frosting

1. Heat oven to 350°F (325°F for dark or nonstick pans). Place paper baking cup in each of 24 regular-size muffin cups.

2. Bake cake mix as directed on box for 24 cupcakes, using water, oil and eggs. Cool 10 minutes; remove from pans to cooling racks. Cool completely, about 30 minutes.

3. Meanwhile, line 2 cookie sheets with waxed paper. In large bowl, place cereal. In 4-quart saucepan, melt butter over low heat. Add marshmallows; stir until completely melted. Remove from heat. Stir in orange food color. Pour marshmallow mixture over cereal in bowl, stirring until well coated.

4. For feet, place 2 gummy candies on cookie sheet. Spray inside of ¼-cup measuring cup with cooking spray. For body, fill measuring cup with warm cereal mixture; place over feet, releasing cereal mixture and covering back half of feet. Repeat with remaining gummy candies and cereal mixture to make 24 aliens. Use 2 candy-coated chocolate candies for eyes and black decorating gel to make centers of eyes. Insert 2 pretzels for antennae.

5. Stir green food color into frosting container; frost cupcakes with frosting. Place 1 alien on top of each cupcake; press gently to secure. Store uncovered at room temperature.

1 Serving: Calories 330; Total Fat 9g (Saturated Fat 3g); Sodium 250mg; Total Carbohydrate 59g (Dietary Fiber 1g); Protein 2g **Exchanges:** 1½ Starch, 2½ Other Carbohydrate, 1½ Fat **Carbohydrate Choices:** 4

Halloween Cupcakes

PREP TIME: 30 Minutes • **START TO FINISH:** 3 Hours 10 Minutes • **24 servings (1 cupcake)**

Cake

1 **box white cake mix with pudding in the mix**

Water, oil and egg whites called for on cake mix package

Frosting and Decorations

1 **container (1 lb) creamy white ready-to-spread frosting**

1 **container (1 lb) chocolate creamy ready-to-spread frosting Neon green food color**

20 **large marshmallows**

¼ **cup coarse black sparkling sugar**

8 **licorice wheels**

6 **sour punch straws (any red flavor)**

16 **small black gumdrops**

Green food color

32 **miniature semisweet chocolate chips**

Black decorating gel

1 **roll chewy fruit flavored snack**

1. Heat oven to 350°F (325°F for dark or nonstick pans). Place paper baking cup in each of 24 muffin cups. Make and bake cake as directed on box for cupcakes, using water, oil and egg whites. Cool completely.

2. Remove lid and foil cover from container of white frosting. In small bowl, reserve ⅓ of white frosting. Microwave remaining white frosting in container uncovered on High about 20 seconds or until frosting can be stirred smooth. Divide warm frosting between 2 small bowls. Reserve ⅓ cup chocolate frosting in small microwavable bowl; set aside. Decorate cupcakes as directed below.

1 Serving: Calories 340 (Calories from Fat 90); Total Fat 9g (Saturated Fat 2.5g); Cholesterol 0mg; Sodium 270mg; Total Carbohydrate 62g (Dietary Fiber 0g); Protein 1g **Exchanges:** 1 Starch, 3 Other Carbohydrate, 1½ Fat **Carbohydrate Choices:** 4

Terrifying Tip

Look for neon food colors next to the standard food colors in the baking ingredients aisle of your supermarket.

Peppermint candy sticks can be substituted for the sour punch straws.

Franken-Cupcakes

Frost 8 cupcakes with chocolate frosting from container. Add 25 drops green food color to warm white frosting in 1 bowl; mix well. Top each cupcake with 1 marshmallow. Spoon 1 tablespoon green frosting over each marshmallow to coat, allowing some frosting to drip onto cupcake top. Press 2 chocolate chips into frosting on each marshmallow for eyes. Use tube of black gel to add a mouth on each marshmallow. Cut fruit snack into pieces; place on top of frosted marshmallow for hair.

Boo-Cupcakes

Frost 8 cupcakes with chocolate frosting from container. Top each cupcake with 1 marshmallow. Rewarm white frosting in microwave 2 to 5 seconds, if necessary. Spoon 1 tablespoon warm frosting from second bowl over each marshmallow to coat, allowing some frosting to drip onto cupcake top. Press 2 chocolate chips into frosting on each marshmallow for eyes.

Witchy-Poo Cupcakes

Add 5 drops neon green food color to reserved white frosting; mix well. Frost 8 cupcakes with green frosting. Microwave reserved chocolate frosting uncovered on High 15 seconds or until frosting can be stirred smooth. Cut 4 marshmallows in half diagonally; shape each half into cone for top of witch's hat. Place toothpick in pointed end of cone. Dip each cone in warm chocolate frosting; cool slightly. Roll cones in black sugar to coat completely. Place 1 licorice wheel on 1 side of each cupcake top for base of witch's hat; place 1 sugarcoated cone on each licorice wheel. Remove toothpicks. Cut each sour punch straw into thirds. Shape each gumdrop into "shoe" and attach each to one end of straw piece. Insert 2 straw "legs" in each cupcake on opposite side of hat.

Friendly Ghost Cupcakes

PREP TIME: 35 Minutes ● **START TO FINISH: 1 Hour 25 Minutes** ● **24 servings (1 cupcake)**

Cake

3	cups Original Bisquick® mix
1	cup granulated sugar
1	cup packed brown sugar
¼	cup butter or margarine, softened
2	teaspoons pumpkin pie spice
¼	cup milk
4	eggs
1	can (15 oz) pumpkin (not pumpkin pie mix)

Frosting and Decorations

1	package (3 oz) cream cheese, softened
½	cup butter or margarine, softened
2	teaspoons vanilla
4½	cups powdered sugar
2	teaspoons miniature chocolate chips

1. Heat oven to 350°F. Line 24 regular-size muffin cups with paper baking cups.

2. In large bowl, beat Bisquick mix, granulated sugar, brown sugar, ¼ cup butter, the pumpkin pie spice, milk, eggs and pumpkin with electric mixer on low speed 30 seconds. Beat on medium speed 3 minutes. Divide batter evenly among muffin cups.

3. Bake 25 to 30 minutes or until toothpick inserted in center of cupcake comes out clean. Cool 5 minutes; remove from pan to wire rack. Cool completely, about 30 minutes.

4. Meanwhile, in large bowl, beat cream cheese and ½ cup butter on low speed about 30 seconds or until well blended. Beat in vanilla and 2 cups of the powdered sugar on low speed about 30 seconds or just until mixed, then on high speed about 1 minute or until fluffy. Beat in remaining 2½ cups powdered sugar, ¼ cup at a time, on medium speed. If too soft to mound, add additional powdered sugar, a tablespoon at a time, until desired consistency.

5. Spoon frosting into large resealable plastic food-storage bag; press out air and seal bag. Cut ½-inch tip from lower corner of bag. Squeeze bag to pipe about 2 tablespoons frosting into ghost-shaped mound on each cupcake. Press 2 chocolate chips, flat sides out, into frosting for eyes.

1 Serving: Calories 370; Total Fat 10g (Saturated Fat 4.5g); Sodium 280mg; Total Carbohydrate 66g (Dietary Fiber 0g); Protein 3g **Exchanges:** ½ Starch, 4 Other Carbohydrate, 2 Fat **Carbohydrate Choices:** 4½

Tombstone Cupcakes

PREP TIME: 30 Minutes • **START TO FINISH: 1 Hour 30 Minutes** • **24 servings (1 cupcake)**

Cake

1 box devil's food cake mix with pudding in the mix

Water, vegetable oil and eggs called for on cake mix box

Frosting and Decorations

1 container (1 lb) creamy white ready-to-spread frosting

2 graham cracker rectangles, crushed

2 chocolate graham cracker rectangles, crushed

1 tube (0.68 oz) black decorating gel

12 chocolate creme-filled finger sandwich cookies, cut in half crosswise

1. Heat oven to 350°F. Place black paper baking cup in each of 24 regular-size muffin cups. Make and bake cake mix as directed on box for 24 cupcakes, using water, oil and eggs. Cool 10 minutes; remove from pans to cooling racks. Cool completely, about 30 minutes.

2. Frost cupcakes with white frosting. Sprinkle each with 1 teaspoon graham cracker crumbs to look like dirt. With black decorating gel, pipe desired design on each cookie half. Insert 1 half into each cupcake to look like tombstone.

1 Serving: Calories 257; Total Fat 12g (Saturated Fat 2g); Sodium 261mg; Total Carbohydrate 36g (Dietary Fiber 1g); Protein 2g **Exchanges:** 1 Starch, 1½ Other Carbohydrate, 2 Fat **Carbohydrate Choices:** 2½

Bat Cupcakes

PREP TIME: 1 Hour • **START TO FINISH: 2 Hours 25 Minutes** • **24 servings (1 cupcake)**

Cake

1 box yellow cake mix with pudding in the mix

Water, vegetable oil and eggs called for on cake mix box

Frosting and Decorations

20 drops yellow food color

1 container butter cream whipped ready-to-spread frosting

1 cup semisweet chocolate chips

Pull-apart cherry licorice twists

1. Heat oven to 350°F (325°F for dark or nonstick pan). Place paper baking cup in each of 24 regular-size muffin cups. Make and bake cake mix as directed on box for 24 cupcakes, using water, oil and eggs. Cool in pans 10 minutes; remove from pans to cooling rack. Cool completely, about 30 minutes.

2. Stir food color into frosting until well blended; frost tops of cupcakes.

3. Line large cookie sheet with waxed paper or cooking parchment paper. On another piece of paper, draw and cut out bat shape about 2½x1 inch. Place shape under waxed paper. In small microwavable bowl, place chocolate chips. Microwave uncovered on High 1 minute; stir. Microwave in 15-second increments, stirring after each, until melted and smooth. Place chocolate in small resealable freezer plastic bag; seal. Cut off tiny corner of bag. Squeeze chocolate onto waxed paper to make bat, filling in bat shape underneath as guide and making 24 bats. Cut ¼-inch pieces of licorice; place on each bat for eyes. Refrigerate about 15 minutes or freeze about 5 minutes until set. Peel waxed paper from chocolate. Place 1 chocolate bat on top of each cupcake just before serving. Store loosely covered.

1 Serving: Calories 220; Total Fat 11g (Saturated Fat 3.5g); Sodium 150mg; Total Carbohydrate 28g (Dietary Fiber 0g); Protein 1g **Exchanges:** ½ Starch, 1½ Other Carbohydrate, 2 Fat **Carbohydrate Choices:** 2

Terrifying Tip

The cupcakes can be made several days ahead and frozen until 2 hours before decorating.

Candy Corn Baby Cakes

PREP TIME: 30 Minutes • **START TO FINISH: 1 Hour 15 Minutes** • **48 servings (1 baby cake)**

Cake

- 1 box white cake mix with pudding

  Water, vegetable oil and egg whites called for on cake mix box

- 1 teaspoon orange paste food color

- 1 teaspoon yellow paste food color

Frosting and Decorations

- 2 containers (1 lb each) creamy white ready-to-spread frosting

  Orange and yellow coarse sugar

- 48 pieces candy corn

1. Heat oven to 350°F (325°F for dark or nonstick pans). Place mini paper baking cup in each of 48 mini muffin cups. Make cake as directed on box for cupcakes, using water, oil and egg whites.

2. Divide batter evenly among 3 medium bowls (about 1½ cups in each). Stir orange food color into one bowl; stir yellow food color into second bowl. Leave remaining batter white. Place about 1 teaspoon of each color batter into each muffin cup, layering colors in order of candy corn—yellow, orange and white. Do not stir! Each muffin cup will be about three-fourths full.

3. Bake 15 minutes or until toothpick inserted in center comes out clean. Cool 10 minutes; remove cupcakes from pans to cooling racks. Cool completely, about 20 minutes.

4. Spread frosting on cupcakes. Sprinkle with coarse sugar; top with candy corn.

1 Serving: Calories 151; Total Fat 6g (Saturated Fat 1g); Sodium 120mg; Total Carbohydrate 24g (Dietary Fiber 0g); Protein 1g **Exchanges:** 1½ Other Carbohydrate, 1 Fat **Carbohydrate Choices:** 1½

Terrifying Tip

Make quick work of filling the mini muffin cups by using a small cookie scoop or measuring teaspoon.

Creepy Crawler Cupcakes

PREP TIME: 25 Minutes • **START TO FINISH: 1 Hour 15 Minutes** • **24 servings (1 cupcake)**

Cake

½	cup unsweetened baking cocoa
1	cup hot water
1⅔	cups all-purpose flour
1½	cups sugar
½	teaspoon baking powder
1	teaspoon baking soda
½	teaspoon salt
½	cup shortening
2	eggs

Frosting and Decorations

1	container (1 lb) chocolate creamy ready-to-spread frosting
	Candy rocks, if desired
24	gummy worms

1. Heat oven to 400°F. Place paper baking cups in 24 regular-size muffin cups. In small bowl, mix cocoa and water with spoon until smooth; cool.

2. In large bowl, beat cooled cocoa mixture and remaining cake ingredients with electric mixer on low speed 2 minutes, scraping bowl constantly. Beat on medium speed 2 minutes, scraping bowl frequently. Fill muffin cups half full.

3. Bake 15 to 20 minutes or until toothpick inserted in center comes out clean. Cool completely, about 30 minutes.

4. Spread frosting on cupcakes. Sprinkle with candy rocks. Add gummy worms, gently pushing one end into cupcake.

1 Serving: Calories 240; Total Fat 9g (Saturated Fat 2.5g); Sodium 180mg; Total Carbohydrate 38g (Dietary Fiber 0g); Protein 2g **Exchanges:** ½ Starch, 2 Other Carbohydrate, 2 Fat **Carbohydrate Choices:** 2½

Terrifying Tip

To make the frosting easier to work with, stir before using.

Crunchy
Peanut Butter Mix,
page 9

Tombstone
Cupcakes,
page 114

Boneyard
Dirt Pops,
page 102

Party Time!

Creating a delightful dessert buffet is an easy and fun way to display an assortment of Halloween treats for party guests or trick-or-treaters.

Refrigerated sugar cookie dough is always great to have on hand. Add some frosting or orange sprinkles to dress up the cookies and use colorful string to stack them.

Display candy and treats in large glass jars with scoops. Be sure to provide treat bags for buffet-goers.

Spiderweb Pull-Apart Cake

PREP TIME: 20 Minutes • **START TO FINISH: 1 Hour 20 Minutes** • **24 servings (1 cupcake)**

Cake

1 **box chocolate cake mix with special dark chocolate syrup and pudding in the mix**

Water, vegetable oil and eggs called for on cake mix box

Frosting and Decorations

3 **containers (1 lb each) vanilla creamy ready-to-spread frosting**

1 **tube (0.68 oz) black decorating gel**

Gummy spider candies

1. Heat oven to 350°F. Place paper baking cup in each of 24 regular-size muffin cups. Make and bake cake mix as directed on box for cupcakes, using water, oil and eggs. Cool 10 minutes; remove from pans to cooling racks. Cool completely, about 30 minutes.

2. Fit #10 tip in decorating bag and fill with 2 containers frosting. Arrange cupcakes on platter, fitting snugly together in spiderweb design. Use tip, with smooth side facing up, to generously pipe frosting over cupcakes. Using spatula, spread frosting smoothly over cupcakes. Fit #862 star tip in decorating bag and fill with remaining container frosting. Generously pipe frosting around edge of spiderweb shape.

3. Using black gel, pipe concentric circles on cake, starting from center and moving toward edge. Pull toothpick through lines of gel 14 to 16 times to create spiderweb. Top with spider candies.

1 Serving: Calories 396; Total Fat 19g (Saturated Fat 5g); Sodium 255mg; Total Carbohydrate 53g (Dietary Fiber 0.5g); Protein 2g **Exchanges:** 3½ Other Carbohydrate, 3 Fat **Carbohydrate Choices:** 3½

Creeping Centipede Cake

PREP TIME: 20 Minutes • **START TO FINISH: 2 Hours 20 Minutes** • **12 servings**

Cake

1 box chocolate fudge cake mix with pudding

Water, vegetable oil and eggs called for on cake mix box

Frosting and Decorations

22 to 25 drops green food color

1½ cups creamy white ready-to-spread frosting (from two 1-lb containers)

1 package (3.5 oz) coconut-and-marshmallow-covered chocolate cake with creamy filling

Black pull-apart licorice twists, cut into 3-inch pieces

2 candy-coated sunflower seeds

3 candy-coated milk chocolate candies

2 cups finely crushed creme-filled chocolate sandwich cookies (15 cookies)

1. Heat oven to 350°F. Spray bottom and sides of 12-cup fluted tube cake pan with cooking spray. Make cake as directed on box, using water, oil and eggs. Pour batter into pan. Bake as directed on box. Cool 10 minutes. Run knife around side of pan to loosen cake; remove from pan to cooling rack. Cool completely, about 1 hour.

2. Cut cake in half vertically. On serving tray, place cake halves, bottom side down. Stir food color into frosting. Place cake halves together end to end, to form S shape. Attach coconut-and-marshmallow cake to front and back of cake with 2 tablespoons frosting. Spread remaining frosting over cake halves. On both sides of bottom half of cake, insert licorice pieces 1½ inches apart for legs. Insert 2 licorice pieces in top of head for antennae. Attach sunflower seeds to antennae with dab of frosting. Add candies for eyes and nose, and licorice pieces for eyebrows and mouth. Place crushed cookies around sides of centipede to look like dirt. Store loosely covered at room temperature.

1 Serving: Calories 478; Total Fat 21.5g (Saturated Fat 3.5g); Sodium 514mg; Total Carbohydrate 67g (Dietary Fiber 1.5g); Protein 4g **Exchanges:** 4½ Other Carbohydrate, ½ Medium-Fat Meat, 3½ Fat **Carbohydrate Choices:** 4½

Terrifying Tip

Use your imagination to make this centipede fun or slightly scary with the use of different candies and food colors.

Wicked Witch Cake

PREP TIME: 40 Minutes • **START TO FINISH: 2 Hours 15 Minutes** • **12 servings**

Cake

1 box yellow cake mix with pudding in the mix

Water, vegetable oil and eggs called for on cake mix box

⅓ cup Halloween multicolored candy sprinkles

Frosting and Decorations

1 container vanilla creamy ready-to-spread frosting

⅛ teaspoon plus 8 drops green food color

1 waffle cone

Betty Crocker® Easy Flow black decorating icing (from 6.4-oz can)

Assorted large gumdrops

3 pieces candy corn

1. Heat oven to 350°F (325°F for dark or nonstick pan). Spray bottom only of 13x9-inch pan with cooking spray. Make cake batter as directed on box, using water, oil and eggs. With rubber spatula, fold in candy sprinkles. Pour batter into pan. Bake as directed on box for 13x9-inch pan. Cool completely, about 1 hour.

2. In small bowl, mix frosting and ⅛ teaspoon green food color until well blended. Spread frosting over cake. To form witch's hat, insert waffle cone at an angle into top center of cake until rounded edge is level with surface of cake. Tip of cone should be raised about 2 inches directly above top edge of cake pan.

3. With toothpick, make 5-inch-long oval outline of witch's face directly below "hat." Immediately drop 8 drops green food color randomly over surface of frosting, avoiding "witch's face"; swirl with knife.

4. Using ribbon tip, frost "witch's hat" with black icing; add a "brim" around the base of the "hat" and frost small areas below her face to look like a cape.

5. Cut and shape gum drops as desired to look like eyebrows, eyes, a nose, a mouth, a hat buckle and cape buttons. Add candy corn to look like teeth. Use drawing tip in black icing to draw witch's hair. Store loosely covered.

1 Serving: Calories 410; Total Fat 18g (Saturated Fat 3.5g); Sodium 350mg; Total Carbohydrate 59g (Dietary Fiber 0g); Protein 2g **Exchanges:** ½ Starch, 3½ Other Carbohydrate, 3½ Fat **Carbohydrate Choices:** 4

Bride of Frankenstein Cake

PREP TIME: 40 Hours • **START TO FINISH: 2 Hours 35 Minutes** • **12 servings**

Cake

1 box white cake mix with pudding in the mix

Water, vegetable oil and egg whites called for on cake mix box

Frosting and Decorations

1 container fluffy white whipped ready-to-spread frosting

4 drops green food color

1 can (6 oz) white decorating icing

1 can (6 oz) blue decorating icing

3 large green gumdrops

2 large white gumdrops

1 tube (0.68 oz) green decorating gel

1 tube (0.68 oz) red decorating gel

1 tube (0.68 oz) black decorating gel

1. Heat oven to 350°F (325°F for dark or nonstick pans). Spray two 9x5-inch loaf pans with cooking spray. Make cake batter as directed on box, using water, oil and egg whites; pour into pans. Bake 32 to 40 minutes or until toothpick inserted in center comes out clean. Cool 10 minutes; remove from pans to cooling rack. Cool completely, about 1 hour.

2. Trim about ¼ inch off top of each cake to level. On long serving platter (at least 18 inches), place cakes bottom sides up to make long rectangle.

3. In small bowl, mix ⅓ cup of the frosting and the green food color until well blended. Frost one-fourth of cake (top and sides) with green frosting for face. Frost remaining cake with remaining white frosting.

4. Using ribbon tips on decorating icing cans, draw alternating white and blue lines, beginning at edge of green frosting, to far end of cake.

5. Place 1 green gumdrop on each side of face for ears and 1 for nose. For eyes, press white gumdrops, small ends down, on face. Use decorating gels for eye pupils, eye lashes, nose and lips. Store loosely covered.

1 Serving (Cake and Frosting Only): Calories 490; Total Fat 19g (Saturated Fat 3.5g); Sodium 350mg; Total Carbohydrate 77g (Dietary Fiber 0g); Protein 2g **Exchanges:** 1½ Starch, 3½ Other Carbohydrate, 3½ Fat **Carbohydrate Choices:** 5

Terrifying Tip

The cake is easier to work with if you freeze it before cutting and decorating.

Halloween Cake

PREP TIME: 40 Minutes • **START TO FINISH: 4 Hours 20 Minutes** • **24 servings**

Cake

2 boxes carrot or spice cake mix with pudding in the mix

   Water, vegetable oil and eggs called for on cake mix boxes

Frosting and Decorations

2 containers vanilla creamy ready-to-spread frosting

   Yellow and red food colors

   Pull-apart green licorice twists

   Chewy fruit-flavored snack rolls (any flavor)

   Edible glitter, if desired

1. Heat oven to 325°F. Spray 2½-quart ovenproof bowl with baking spray with flour. In large bowl, make 1 box of cake batter as directed on box, using water, oil and eggs. Pour batter into ovenproof bowl. Bake 1 hour 15 minutes to 1 hour 20 minutes or until toothpick inserted in center comes out clean. Cool 15 minutes. Run knife just around top edge of cake. Remove cake from bowl; place rounded side up on cooling rack. Repeat with remaining box of cake mix to make second cake. Cool cakes completely, about 1 hour.

2. In medium bowl, tint frosting with 9 drops yellow and 6 drops red food color to make orange frosting. Trim bottoms of both cakes to form flat surfaces. Place 1 cake, round side down, on plate. Spread ⅔ cup of the orange frosting over flat side of cake almost to edge. Place second cake, round side up, on frosted cake to make round shape. Frost entire cake with remaining orange frosting.

3. To make stem, cut twist of licorice crosswise into thirds. Gather pieces together and twist. Use toothpick to make hole in top of cake; insert licorice stem. Pull apart licorice to make vines. Cut leaves from fruit snack rolls. Garnish cake with vines and leaves. Sprinkle with glitter. Store loosely covered.

1 Serving (Cake and Frosting Only): Calories 410; Total Fat 20g (Saturated Fat 4g); Sodium 350mg; Potassium 55mg; Total Carbohydrate 54g (Dietary Fiber 0g); Protein 3g **Exchanges:** 1 Starch, 2½ Other Carbohydrate, 4 Fat **Carbohydrate Choices:** 3½

Terrifying Tip

Instead of licorice, use a green flat-bottom ice cream cone for a stem, placing it upside down.

Graveyard Cake

PREP TIME: 55 Minutes • **START TO FINISH: 1 Hour 20 Minutes** • **24 servings**

Cake

1   **box yellow cake mix with pudding in the mix**

    Water, vegetable oil and eggs called for on cake mix box

Frosting and Decorations

¼   **cup chocolate-flavored candy melts or coating wafers, melted**

2 to 3 **oval creme-filled or peanut-shaped peanut butter–filled sandwich cookies, each cut in half crosswise**

1   **container vanilla creamy ready-to-spread frosting**

20 **drops neon green food color**

5   **rectangular graham crackers**

2   **rectangular chocolate graham crackers**

    Candy-coated peanut butter pieces

    Candy corn

    Candy pumpkins

1. Heat oven to 350°F. Spray 15x10x1-inch pan with cooking spray. Make cake batter as directed on box, using water, oil and eggs. Pour batter into pan; spread evenly. Bake 17 to 22 minutes or until toothpick inserted in center comes out clean. Cool completely in pan, about 30 minutes.

2. Meanwhile, place sheet of foil on cookie sheet. Spoon melted candy melts into small resealable food-storage plastic bag; seal bag. Cut small hole in corner of bag. Squeeze melted candy in shape of tree onto foil. Refrigerate tree. Squeeze melted candy on sandwich cookies to look like tombstones.

3. In small bowl, mix frosting and food color until blended. Reserve ¼ cup frosting for roof and decorations. Frost cake with remaining frosting. With sharp knife, cut peaks in one short side of each of 2 graham crackers. Insert crackers into cake for front and back of haunted house. Break 1 graham cracker in half crosswise; insert into cake for sides of house. Frost 2 graham crackers; place on house for roof.

4. Break up 1 chocolate graham cracker; arrange on cake for walkway and on house for windows and door. Arrange peanut butter pieces along walkway. Pipe frosting along top of house; arrange candy corn in frosting. Arrange chocolate tree, candy pumpkins and "tombstones" on cake. Crush remaining chocolate graham cracker; mound graham cracker crumbs in front of tombstones.

1 Serving (Cake and Frosting Only): Calories 190; Total Fat 9g (Saturated Fat 2g); Sodium 180mg; Potassium 25mg; Total Carbohydrate 28g (Dietary Fiber 0g); Protein 1g **Exchanges:** ½ Starch, 1½ Other Carbohydrate, 1½ Fat **Carbohydrate Choices:** 2

Spiderweb Applesauce Cake

PREP TIME: 30 Minutes • **START TO FINISH: 2 Hours 5 Minutes** • **24 servings**

Cake

2	cups all-purpose flour
1	cup granulated sugar
1	cup packed brown sugar
2	teaspoons baking powder
1	teaspoon baking soda
1	teaspoon ground cinnamon
1	cup vegetable oil
1	cup applesauce
1	teaspoon vanilla
4	eggs

Frosting and Decorations

1	container (1 lb) caramel ready-to-spread frosting
¼	cup vanilla creamy ready-to-spread frosting
24	brown candy-coated peanut butter candies
24	brown miniature candy-coated chocolate baking bits
2	tablespoons chocolate creamy ready-to-spread frosting

1. Heat oven to 350°F. Grease bottom and sides of 15x10x1-inch pan with shortening or cooking spray.

2. In large bowl, mix flour, sugars, baking powder, baking soda and cinnamon. Add oil, applesauce, vanilla and eggs; beat with electric mixer on low speed until smooth. Spread in pan.

3. Bake 28 to 32 minutes or until toothpick inserted in center comes out clean and surface is deep golden brown. Cool completely, about 1 hour.

4. Frost with dulce de leche frosting. Cut into 6 rows by 4 rows, but leave in pan.

5. To decorate, spoon vanilla frosting into resealable food-storage plastic bag; seal bag and cut off 1 tiny corner. Pipe vanilla frosting in a spiral in corner where 4 squares meet (see photo). Pull a toothpick from corner of each square through lines of frosting 4 to 5 times to create spiderweb. Repeat to make 6 webs.

6. Place 1 peanut butter candy and 1 baking bit next to spider web on each square. Spoon chocolate frosting into another resealable food-storage plastic bag; seal bag and cut off 1 tiny corner. Pipe chocolate frosting to make 6 legs for each spider.

1 Serving: Calories 320; Total Fat 15g (Saturated Fat 3g); Sodium 170mg; Total Carbohydrate 43g (Dietary Fiber 0g); Protein 2g **Exchanges:** 3 Other Carbohydrate, 3 Fat **Carbohydrate Choices:** 3

Terrifying Tip

Dulce de leche refers to a rich, sweet, caramelized milk that's popular in Latin America.

Brownie Pumpkin Cheesecake

PREP TIME: 15 Minutes • **START TO FINISH:** 4 Hours 10 Minutes • **12 servings**

Brownie Base

1 box (1 lb 2.3 oz) dark chocolate fudge brownie mix

Water, vegetable oil and eggs called for on brownie mix box

Filling

2 packages (8 oz each) cream cheese, softened

½ cup sugar

½ cup canned pumpkin (not pumpkin pie mix)

2 eggs

½ teaspoon vanilla

½ teaspoon pumpkin pie spice

½ cup semisweet chocolate chips, melted

1. Heat oven to 350°F. Spray 10-inch springform pan with cooking spray. Make brownie batter as directed on box for basic recipe, using water, oil and eggs; spread in pan. Bake 28 to 30 minutes or until toothpick inserted 2 inches from side of pan comes out almost clean.

2. Meanwhile, in large bowl, beat cream cheese and sugar with electric mixer on medium speed until smooth and creamy. Beat in pumpkin until well blended. On low speed, beat in eggs 1 at a time, just until combined. Stir in vanilla and pumpkin pie spice. Reserve ½ cup filling in small bowl. Pour remaining filling over baked brownie base.

3. Stir melted chocolate into reserved filling; place chocolate in large resealable food-storage plastic bag. Seal bag; cut off 1 corner of bag. Squeeze bag to pipe jack-o'-lantern face on cheesecake.

4. Bake 40 to 45 minutes or until center is almost set. Cool 30 minutes. Run knife around edge of pan to loosen cheesecake. Cool 30 minutes longer. Refrigerate at least 2 hours before serving. Cover and refrigerate any remaining cheesecake.

1 Serving: Calories 510; Total Fat 29g (Saturated Fat 11g); Sodium 290mg; Total Carbohydrate 55g (Dietary Fiber 2g); Protein 7g **Exchanges:** 1½ Starch, 2½ Other Carbohydrate, ½ High-Fat Meat, 5 Fat **Carbohydrate Choices:** 3½

Terrifying Tip

Using dark chocolate chips in the filling will give this cheesecake a richer chocolate flavor.

Dirt Ice Cream Cake

PREP TIME: 25 Minutes • **START TO FINISH: 3 Hours 55 Minutes** • **24 servings**

½ gallon (8 cups) cookies 'n cream ice cream, softened

1 box devil's food cake mix with pudding in the mix

Water, vegetable oil and eggs called for on cake mix box

1 box (6-serving size) chocolate instant pudding and pie filling mix

2 cups milk

20 creme-filled chocolate sandwich cookies, crushed

1 package (8.4 oz) gummy worm candies

1. Line bottom and sides of 13x9-inch pan with waxed paper, leaving about 2 inches of waxed paper overhanging all sides of pan. Press ice cream evenly in pan. Cover with plastic wrap; freeze 2 hours or until firm.

2. Heat oven to 350°F. Grease bottom only of another 13x9-inch pan with shortening or cooking spray; line pan with cooking parchment paper. Make and bake cake mix as directed on box, using water, oil and eggs. Cool 10 minutes; run knife around side of pan to loosen. Place cooling rack upside down over pan; turn rack and pan over. Remove pan and paper. Cool cake completely, about 1 hour.

3. Beat pudding mix and milk with wire whisk 2 minutes; let stand 3 minutes. Cover; refrigerate 1 hour.

4. Split cake horizontally to make 2 layers. Return bottom layer of cake to pan. Use waxed paper to lift ice cream from pan. Place ice cream on top of cake layer; top with remaining cake layer.

5. Spread pudding evenly on cake. Sprinkle with cookie crumbs and gummy worm candies. Serve immediately. Store covered in freezer.

1 Serving: Calories 360; Total Fat 16g (Saturated Fat 6g); Sodium 313mg; Total Carbohydrate 52g (Dietary Fiber 1g); Protein 5g **Exchanges:** 3 Other Carbohydrate, ½ Milk, 2 Fat **Carbohydrate Choices:** 3½

Mini Pumpkin Cakes

PREP TIME: 30 Minutes • **START TO FINISH: 1 Hour 35 Minutes** •
6 servings (1 mini pumpkin cake)

Cake

1 box spice cake mix with pudding in the mix

Water, vegetable oil and eggs called for on cake mix box

Frosting and Decorations

2 containers (1 lb each) vanilla creamy ready-to-spread frosting

Yellow and red food color

Green sour straws, cut into 1-inch pieces

6 green gumdrops

1. Heat oven to 350°F. Grease 2 miniature fluted tube cake pans with shortening; lightly flour. Make cake mix as directed on box for cupcakes, using water, oil and eggs. Divide batter evenly among cake pans.

2. Bake 22 to 25 minutes or until toothpick inserted in center comes out clean. Cool 10 minutes; remove cakes from pans to cooling racks. Cool completely, about 30 minutes.

3. In medium bowl, tint frosting with 2 teaspoons yellow food color and 1 teaspoon red food color to make orange frosting.

4. Trim bottom of each cake to form flat surfaces. For each pumpkin cake, place 1 cake, rounded side down, on plate. Top with second cake, rounded side up. Frost entire cake with orange frosting, filling center with frosting.

5. Insert sour straw piece into each cake for stem. On work surface, flatten gumdrops with rolling pin; with small paring knife, cut out leaf shapes. Decorate cakes with gumdrop leaves.

1 Serving: Calories 1,169; Total Fat 49g (Saturated Fat 14g); Sodium 756mg; Total Carbohydrate 168g (Dietary Fiber 0g); Protein 7g **Exchanges:** 2 Starch, 9 Other Carbohydrate, 10 Fat **Carbohydrate Choices:** 11

Terrifying Tip
Use green icing to make vines on pumpkins, if desired.

Frightful Cookies & Other Treats

Forget about tricks—these sweet treats will scare you silly!

Caramel-Apple Biscuit Pops

PREP TIME: 15 Minutes • **START TO FINISH: 40 Minutes** • **12 servings (1 biscuit pop)**

Biscuit Cups

- 1 can (16.3 oz) Pillsbury® Grands!® refrigerated buttermilk biscuits
- 2 tablespoons butter or margarine, melted
- 1 medium apple, peeled, chopped (1 cup)
- 3 tablespoons granulated sugar
- 1 teaspoon ground cinnamon
- 12 paper lollipop sticks

Icing

- ½ cup packed brown sugar
- ¼ cup whipping cream
- ¾ cup powdered sugar

1. Heat oven to 350°F. Place paper baking cup in each of 12 regular-size muffin cups. Cut each biscuit into 6 pieces; place in large bowl. Add butter, apple, granulated sugar and cinnamon; toss gently to mix. Spoon mixture into muffin cups.

2. Bake 20 to 25 minutes or until golden brown. Immediately remove from pan.

3. Meanwhile, in 1-quart saucepan, heat brown sugar and whipping cream to full rolling boil over medium heat, stirring constantly. Remove from heat. Beat in powdered sugar until smooth.

4. Spoon warm icing over warm biscuit cups. Insert lollipop stick into center of each cup.

1 Serving: Calories 240; Total Fat 9g (Saturated Fat 4g); Sodium 420mg; Total Carbohydrate 37g (Dietary Fiber 0g); Protein 3g **Exchanges:** 1 Starch, 1½ Other Carbohydrate, 1½ Fat **Carbohydrate Choices:** 2½

Terrifying Tip

Skip the sticks and make it a biscuit cup—
just as delicious!

Halloween Party Pops

PREP TIME: 1 Hour 15 Minutes • START TO FINISH: 2 Hours 15 Minutes • 16 cookie pops

Cookies

- 1 roll (16.5 oz) Pillsbury® refrigerated sugar cookies
- 16 flat wooden sticks with rounded ends

White Frosting

- 1 cup powdered sugar
- 1 tablespoon milk
- 1 tablespoon butter or margarine, softened

Chocolate Frosting

- 1 cup powdered sugar
- 2 tablespoons unsweetened baking cocoa
- 1 to 2 tablespoons milk
- 1 tablespoon butter or margarine, softened

  Assorted candies (gumdrops, candy sprinkles, etc.)

1. Freeze cookie dough for 1 hour.

2. Heat oven to 350°F. Cut frozen dough into 16 (½-inch) slices; roll each into ball. Arrange in circle on ungreased cookie sheets, 3 inches apart and 2 inches from edges. Securely insert a wooden stick into each ball with end pointing toward center of cookie sheet.

3. Bake 10 to 14 minutes or until golden brown. Cool 2 minutes; remove from cookie sheet to cooling rack. Cool completely, about 15 minutes.

4. In small bowl, mix white frosting ingredients until smooth. If necessary, add additional milk 1 drop at a time for desired consistency.

5. In another small bowl, mix all chocolate frosting ingredients except assorted candies until smooth. If necessary, add additional milk 1 drop at a time for desired consistency.

6. Frost half of cookies with white frosting; frost remaining cookies with chocolate frosting. Arrange candies on frosted cookies to create jack-o'-lanterns, cats, owls or ghosts.

1 Cookie Pop: Calories 250; Total Fat 7g (Saturated Fat 2.5g); Sodium 95mg; Total Carbohydrate 45g (Dietary Fiber 0g); Protein 1g **Exchanges:** 3 Other Carbohydrate, 1½ Fat **Carbohydrate Choices:** 3

% Daily Value: Vitamin A 0%; Vitamin C 0%; Calcium 0%; Iron 4%

BLACK CAT COOKIE POPS

To make Black Cat Cookie Pops, frost cookies with orange frosting (use drops of red and yellow food color). For each cookie, slice a large black gumdrop into 3 round pieces. Use small end for head; use largest piece for body. Cut ears and tail from third piece. Arrange gumdrop pieces on frosted cookie to form cat.

SPIDERWEB COOKIES

For Spiderweb Cookies, use white and chocolate frosting. Frost cookies with chocolate frosting. Place white frosting in small resealable food-storage plastic bag; partially seal bag. Cut small hole in bottom corner of bag. Squeeze bag in spiral pattern, starting from center of cookie. Starting at center, pull edge of knife outward through frosting at intervals to make web design.

Peanut Butter Spider Cookies

PREP TIME: 1 Hour • **START TO FINISH: 1 Hour** • **3 dozen cookies**

1 pouch peanut butter cookie mix

3 tablespoons vegetable oil

1 tablespoon water

1 egg

36 round chewy caramels in milk chocolate (from 12-oz bag), unwrapped

Black or red string licorice

⅓ cup (72) miniature candy-coated milk chocolate baking bits

1 tube (0.68 oz) black decorating gel

1. Heat oven to 375°F. In medium bowl, stir cookie mix, oil, water and egg until dough forms.

2. Shape dough into 36 (1-inch) balls. Place 2 inches apart on ungreased cookie sheets.

3. Bake 8 to 10 minutes or until light golden brown. Immediately press 1 chewy caramel in center of each cookie. Cool 2 minutes; remove from cookie sheets to cooling racks.

4. Cut licorice into 8 (2-inch) pieces for each spider. Attach legs by sticking into chewy caramel. Use baking bits for eyes and black gel to make pupils of eyes. Store in single layer tightly covered.

1 Cookie: Calories: 120; Total Fat 4.5g (Saturated Fat 1g); Sodium 95mg; Total Carbohydrate 18g (Dietary Fiber 0g); Protein 1g **Exchanges**: 1 Other Carbohydrate, 1 Fat **Carbohydrate Choices**: 1

Chocolate Mocha Mummy Cookies

PREP TIME: 1 Hour 10 Minutes • **START TO FINISH: 1 Hour 40 Minutes** • **20 servings (1 cookie)**

Cookies

- 1 **cup butter or margarine, softened**
- 1 **cup powdered sugar**
- 1 **teaspoon vanilla**
- 1¾ **cups all-purpose flour**
- ⅓ **cup unsweetened baking cocoa**
- 1 **teaspoon instant coffee granules or crystals**

Decorations

- 1¼ **cups white vanilla baking chips**
- 40 **miniature candy-coated milk chocolate baking bits (about ¼ cup)**

1. In large bowl, beat butter, powdered sugar and vanilla with electric mixer on medium speed 2 minutes or until creamy. On low speed, beat in flour, cocoa and coffee granules 1 to 2 minutes or until well blended. Divide dough into 2 balls; press each to form disk. Wrap each disk in plastic wrap; freeze 10 minutes.

2. Heat oven to 350°F. On lightly floured surface, roll 1 dough disk to ⅛-inch thickness. Cut with 5-inch gingerbread boy cutter. On ungreased cookie sheets, place cutouts 1 inch apart. Repeat with second dough disk. Reroll scraps and cut out additional cookies.

3. Bake 9 to 10 minutes or until set. Cool 1 minute; remove from cookie sheets to cooling racks. Cool completely, about 20 minutes.

4. In small resealable plastic freezer bag, place baking chips; seal bag. Microwave on High 30 seconds. Turn bag over; microwave 15 seconds longer until chips are softened. Squeeze bag until chips are smooth. Cut off tiny corner of bag. Squeeze bag to drizzle melted chips over cookies for mummy wrapping. Add 2 candies to each cookie for eyes.

1 Serving: Calories 220; Total Fat 13g (Saturated Fat 8g); Sodium 75mg; Total Carbohydrate 23g (Dietary Fiber 1g); Protein 2g **Exchanges:** 1½ Other Carbohydrate, 2½ Fat **Carbohydrate Choices:** 1½

Terrifying Tip

Use purchased white frosting instead of melting the white chips. There's no need to melt the frosting; just spoon into a small resealable food-storage plastic bag and pipe it on the cookies.

Chocolate Bat Cookies

PREP TIME: 55 Minutes • **START TO FINISH: 2 Hours 5 Minutes** • **About 4 dozen cookies**

Cookies

¾	**cup butter**
1⅓	**cups granulated sugar**
1	**egg**
1	**teaspoon vanilla**
1½	**cups all-purpose flour**
¾	**cup unsweetened baking cocoa**
⅛	**teaspoon salt**

Decorations

2	**tablespoons red cinnamon candies (96 candies)**
	Black decorator sugar crystals

1. In large bowl, beat butter, granulated sugar, egg and vanilla with electric mixer on medium speed, or mix with spoon. Stir in flour, cocoa and salt. Divide dough in half. Flatten each portion into a disk. Wrap in plastic wrap; refrigerate 1 hour.

2. Heat oven to 375°F. On lightly floured surface, roll one portion of dough at a time ⅛ inch thick. (Keep remaining dough in refrigerator until ready to roll.) Cut with 4½x½-inch bat-shaped cookie cutter. (If dough becomes too sticky to cut, refrigerate 10 minutes before rerolling.) Place 2 red cinnamon candies on each cookie for eyes. Sprinkle with sugar crystals. On ungreased cookie sheet, place cookies about 1 inch apart.

3. Bake 8 to 10 minutes or until edges are set. Cool 1 minute; remove from cookie sheet to cooling rack.

1 Cookie: Calories 70; Total Fat 3.5g (Saturated Fat 1g); Sodium 10mg; Total Carbohydrate 10g (Dietary Fiber 0g); Protein 0g **Exchanges:** ½ Other Carbohydrate, ½ Fat **Carbohydrate Choices:** ½

Terrifying Tips

Outline the edges of the bat with black decorating gel for more detail.

When shopping for black decorator sugar crystals, you might find it labeled as black sanding sugar.

Candy Corn Cookies

PREP TIME: 1 Hour • **START TO FINISH: 2 Hours 30 Minutes** • **About 9 1/2 dozen cookies**

1 **pouch (1 lb 1.5 oz) sugar cookie mix**

⅓ **cup canola oil**

1 **egg**

Orange paste food color

2 **oz semisweet chocolate, melted, cooled**

1. Line 8x4-inch loaf pan with waxed paper, extending paper up over sides of pan. In medium bowl, stir cookie mix, oil and egg until soft dough forms.

2. On work surface, place ¾ cup dough. Knead desired amount of orange food color into dough until color is uniform. Press dough evenly in bottom of pan.

3. Divide remaining dough in half. Gently press one half of remaining dough into pan on top of orange dough. On work surface, knead chocolate into remaining dough until color is uniform. Press over plain dough in pan, pressing gently to edge of pan. Refrigerate 1½ to 2 hours or until firm.

4. Heat oven to 375°F. Remove dough from pan. Cut crosswise into ¼-inch slices. Cut each slice into 5 wedges. On ungreased cookie sheet, place 1 inch apart.

5. Bake 7 to 9 minutes or until cookies are set and edges are very light golden brown. Cool 1 minute; remove from cookie sheet. Cool completely. Store in tightly covered container.

1 Cookie: Calories 25; Total Fat 1g (Saturated Fat 0g); Sodium 15mg; Total Carbohydrate 4g (Dietary Fiber 0g); Protein 0g **Exchanges:** ½ Other Carbohydrate **Carbohydrate Choices:** 0

Terrifying Tip

Paste food color provides intense color without adding liquid to a recipe. Look for it in the baking section of craft or kitchen stores.

Scary Cat Cookies

PREP TIME: 30 Minutes • START TO FINISH: 1 Hour 15 Minutes • About 15 cookies

Cookies

3	oz semisweet baking chocolate
1	cup butter, softened (do not use margarine)
½	cup sugar
2¼	cups all-purpose flour
1	teaspoon vanilla
1	egg

Decorations

	Yellow candy sprinkles
15	miniature candy-coated chocolate baking bits
1	package pull-apart yellow licorice twists, cut into 1-inch pieces
1	package pull-apart pink licorice twists, cut into bits

1. Heat oven to 350°F. Grease cookie sheets with shortening.

2. In small saucepan, melt chocolate over low heat, stirring constantly. In large bowl, beat butter and sugar with electric mixer on medium speed, or mix with spoon. Stir in melted chocolate, flour, vanilla and egg.

3. Shape dough into 30 (1-inch) balls. Pull a little bit of dough from each of 15 balls to make tails; set aside. Cut about ¼-inch slit in same balls, using scissors. Separate dough at slit for cat's ears. Place balls about 2 inches apart on cookie sheets.

4. Place remaining balls below each cat head on cookie sheets for body. Shape small pieces of dough into 15 (2 ½-inch-long) ropes. Place end of rope under each body.

5. Bake 12 to 14 minutes or until set. Remove from cookie sheets to cooling racks. Cool 30 minutes.

6. Use sprinkles to make eyes and baking bits to make noses. Add yellow licorice pieces for whiskers. Add pink licorice for tongues.

1 Cookie: Calories 250; Total Fat 15g (Saturated Fat 9g); Sodium 100mg; Total Carbohydrate 27g (Dietary Fiber 0g); Protein 3g **Exchanges:** 1 Starch, 1 Other Carbohydrate, 2½ Fat **Carbohydrate Choices:** 2

Terrifying Tip

Use a small dab of chocolate frosting, peanut butter or melted chocolate to adhere the candy to the cats' faces.

Gingerbread Skeletons

PREP TIME: 40 Minutes • **START TO FINISH: 2 Hours 10 Minutes** • **18 servings (1 cookie)**

Cookies

- 1 cup packed brown sugar
- ¾ cup butter or margarine, softened
- ½ cup molasses
- 1 egg
- 3 cups all-purpose flour
- 1 teaspoon baking soda
- 2 teaspoons ground ginger
- 2 teaspoons ground cinnamon
- ½ teaspoon salt
- ½ teaspoon ground cloves

Frosting

- 1 container (1 lb) vanilla creamy ready-to-spread frosting

1. In large bowl, beat brown sugar, butter, molasses and egg with electric mixer on medium speed until well blended. On low speed, beat in flour, baking soda, ginger, cinnamon, salt and cloves. Turn dough out onto lightly floured surface; gather into a ball and press into a flat disk. Wrap with plastic wrap; refrigerate 1 hour or until firm.

2. Heat oven to 350°F. Lightly spray cookie sheets with cooking spray. On lightly floured surface, roll dough to ¼-inch thickness. Cut with floured 4- to 5-inch gingerbread man cookie cutter. Place 2 inches apart on cookie sheet. Reroll dough and cut additional cookies.

3. Bake 10 to 12 minutes or until no indentation remains when touched in center. Immediately remove from cookie sheets to cooling racks. Cool completely, about 30 minutes.

4. Remove lid and foil seal from frosting container. Microwave on High 30 seconds; stir until smooth. Spoon frosting into resealable food-storage plastic bag; seal bag. Cut off tiny corner of bag. Twist bag above frosting; squeeze bag to pipe frosting in skeleton design on cookies.

1 Serving: Calories 328; Total Fat 13g (Saturated Fat 6.5g); Sodium 205mg; Total Carbohydrate 49.5g (Dietary Fiber 0.5g); Protein 2.5g **Exchanges:** 1 Starch, 2 Other Carbohydrate, 2½ Fat **Carbohydrate Choices:** 3

Terrifying Tip

This recipe makes a large amount of dough and produces big cookies. You can divide the dough in half; freeze half of the dough up to 3 months, and bake and decorate the cookies as needed.

Spooky Spiderweb Cookie

PREP TIME: 40 Minutes • **START TO FINISH: 1 Hour 20 Minutes** • **16 servings**

Cookies

1	roll (16.5 oz) Pillsbury® refrigerated chocolate chip cookies
⅓	cup unsweetened baking cocoa

Frosting and Decorations

½	cup vanilla creamy ready-to-spread frosting (from 1-lb container)
5	drops red food color
9	drops yellow food color
7	large black gumdrops

1. Heat oven to 350°F. Line 12-inch pizza pan with foil; grease foil. In large bowl, break up cookie dough. Stir or knead in cocoa until well blended. With floured fingers, press dough in pan to form crust. Bake 11 to 13 minutes or until edges are set. Cool completely, about 30 minutes.

2. In 1-quart saucepan over low heat, melt frosting, stirring constantly. Stir in red and yellow food color to make orange color.

3. Place frosting in small resealable food storage plastic bag; partially seal bag. Cut small hole in bottom corner of bag. Squeeze bag in spiral pattern, starting from center of cookie. Starting at center, quickly pull edge of knife outward through frosting at 1-inch intervals to make web design. Let stand 15 minutes or until set.

4. Meanwhile, on generously sugared surface, press 4 gumdrops into 2-inch rounds. Slice each thinly into 6 pieces; roll and shape to resemble spider legs. Place remaining 3 gumdrops on spiderweb to resemble spiders; arrange 8 legs around each spider.

1 Serving: Calories 220; Total Fat 10g (Saturated Fat 3g); Sodium 125mg; Total Carbohydrate 30g (Dietary Fiber 1g); Protein 1g **Exchanges:** 2 Other Carbohydrate, 2 Fat **Carbohydrate Choices:** 2

Terrifying Tips

Make additional spiders, if desired, to decorate the cookies or the table.

If you like, use the microwave to melt the frosting. Place frosting in a small microwavable bowl and microwave on High 15 to 20 seconds or until frosting is thin.

Wickedly Fun Witches

PREP TIME: 40 Minutes • **START TO FINISH: 40 Minutes** • **24 servings (1 cookie)**

Cookies

24   peanut butter–filled sandwich cookies

Frosting and Decorations

½   cup vanilla creamy ready-to-spread frosting (from 1-lb container)

9   drops green food color

4   drops yellow food color

72   miniature candy-coated chocolate baking bits

24   pieces candy corn

3   bars (1.55 oz each) milk chocolate candy

12   chocolate wafer cookies

1. Line cookie sheet with waxed paper. Place sandwich cookies on cookie sheet. In resealable food-storage plastic bag, place frosting and food colors; seal bag. Squeeze bag until frosting is well blended. Cut off tiny corner of bag.

2. Pipe thick line across each sandwich cookie near the top. Pipe 1 large dot of frosting above line on each cookie. Below line, pipe squiggles of frosting to look like witch's hair. On each cookie, pipe 2 dots for eyes, 1 for nose and 1 for mouth. Place miniature candies on dots for eyes and mouth; place candy corn on dot for nose.

3. Cut candy bars crosswise into quarters. Cut each quarter in half to form 2 triangles. Place 1 candy triangle over large dot of frosting on each cookie for top of witch's hat.

4. With serrated knife and sawing motion, cut each chocolate wafer cookie in half. Place cookie half upright on green line at base of each candy triangle for hat brim.

1 Serving: Calories 150; Total Fat 7g (Saturated Fat 2.5g); Sodium 85mg; Total Carbohydrate 21g (Dietary Fiber 0g); Protein 1g **Exchanges:** 1½ Other Carbohydrate, 1½ Fat **Carbohydrate Choices:** 1½

Terrifying Tip

This is a fun no-cook recipe that's ideal for kids to make. Just cut the candy bars and chocolate wafers ahead of time, then let them be creative!

THE·Witchie·Poos

Witches' Brooms

PREP TIME: 35 Minutes • START TO FINISH: 1 Hour 5 Minutes • 20 cookies

½ cup packed brown sugar

½ cup butter or margarine, softened

2 tablespoons water

1 teaspoon vanilla

1½ cups all-purpose flour

⅛ teaspoon salt

10 pretzel rods (about 8 ½ inches long), cut in half crosswise

2 teaspoons shortening

⅔ cup semisweet chocolate chips

⅓ cup butterscotch chips

½ teaspoon shortening

1. Heat oven to 350°F. In medium bowl, beat brown sugar, butter, water and vanilla with electric mixer on medium speed until blended. Stir in flour and salt. Shape dough into 20 (1¼-inch) balls.

2. Place pretzel rod halves on ungreased cookie sheets. Press ball of dough onto cut end of each pretzel rod. Press dough with fork to look like bristles of broom. Bake about 12 minutes or until set but not brown. Remove from cookie sheet to cooling racks. Cool completely.

3. Cover cookie sheet with waxed paper. Place brooms on waxed paper. In 1-quart saucepan, melt 2 teaspoons shortening and the chocolate chips over low heat, stirring occasionally, until smooth. Remove from heat. Spoon melted chocolate over brooms, leaving about 1 inch at top of pretzel handle and bottom halves of cookie bristles uncovered.

4. In small microwavable bowl, microwave butterscotch chips and ½ teaspoon shortening uncovered on Medium-High (70%) 30 to 50 seconds, stirring after 30 seconds, until chips can be stirred smooth. Drizzle over chocolate. Let stand until chocolate is firm before storing.

1 Cookie: Calories 180; Total Fat 8g (Saturated Fat 5g); Sodium 160mg; Total Carbohydrate 24g (Dietary Fiber 1g); Protein 2g **Exchanges:** ½ Starch, 1 Other Carbohydrate, 1½ Fat **Carbohydrate Choices:** 1½

Terrifying Tip

Cookie dough can be covered and refrigerated up to 24 hours before baking. If it's too firm to shape, let it stand at room temperature 30 minutes.

Harvest Moons

1 bag (14 oz) orange candy melts or coating wafers

1 package (24 oz) chocolate-covered marshmallow sandwich pies

Halloween candies and sugar cake decorations, if desired

Decorating icing

Sprinkles, if desired

1. In medium microwavable bowl, microwave candy melts uncovered on Medium (50%) 1 minute, stirring once, until melted. Spoon melted coating into resealable food-storage plastic bag; seal bag. Cut off tiny corner of bag.

2. Pipe border of melted coating around edges of sandwich pies (rewarm coating in microwave, if necessary).

3. Attach candies and cake decorations with icing; decorate with sprinkles. Place on waxed paper; let stand until set.

1 Serving: Calories 411; Total Fat 19g (Saturated Fat 11g); Sodium 124mg; Total Carbohydrate 60g (Dietary Fiber 1g); Protein 4g **Exchanges:** 4 Other Carbohydrate, 3 Fat **Carbohydrate Choices:** 4

HARVEST MOON LOLLIPOPS

To make Harvest Moon Lollipops, insert paper lollipop stick 2 to 3 inches into marshmallow center of each sandwich pie. Pipe melted candy coating where stick meets pie to secure. Lay flat until firm. For a special touch, tie Halloween-patterned ribbon around each lollipop stick.

Jack-o'-Lantern Whoopie Pies

PREP TIME: 30 Minutes • **START TO FINISH: 50 Minutes** • **16 servings**

Cookies

- 1 box spice cake mix with pudding in the mix
- 1 cup canned pumpkin (not pumpkin pie mix)
- ½ cup butter, softened
- ¼ cup milk
- 1 egg
- 1 teaspoon orange gel food color

Filling and Decorations

- ¼ cup butter or margarine, softened
- 4 oz (half of 8-oz package) cream cheese, softened
- 1½ cups powdered sugar
- ½ teaspoon maple flavor extract
- 1 tube (4.25 oz) black decorating icing
- 1 tube (4.25 oz) green decorating icing

1. Heat oven to 375°F. Spray cookie sheets with cooking spray. In large bowl, beat cookie ingredients with electric mixer on medium speed until smooth. Using (2-tablespoon-size) ice cream scoop, drop batter 2 inches apart onto cookie sheets. With damp hands, gently smooth out dough.

2. Bake 12 to 15 minutes or until set. Cool 5 minutes; remove from cookie sheets to cooling racks. Cool completely, about 15 minutes.

3. In medium bowl, beat ¼ cup butter and the cream cheese with electric mixer on medium speed until light and fluffy. Gradually add powdered sugar; beat until blended. Stir in maple extract.

4. For each pie, spread about 1 generous tablespoon filling on bottom of 1 cooled cookie. Top with second cookie, bottom side down; gently press cookies together.

5. Using black decorating icing, pipe jack-o'-lantern faces. Using green decorating icing, pipe jack-o'-lantern stems on tops of pies.

1 Serving: Calories 313; Total Fat 14g (Saturated Fat 8g); Sodium 342mg; Total Carbohydrate 49g (Dietary Fiber 0.5g); Protein 3g **Exchanges:** 1 Starch, 2 Other Carbohydrate, 2½ Fat **Carbohydrate Choices:** 3

Terrifying Tip

The texture of these pies is exceptionally soft. They're best stored tightly covered in the refrigerator.

Chocolate Whoopie Pies

PREP TIME: 1 Hour 30 Minutes • **START TO FINISH: 1 Hour 50 Minutes** • **17 servings (1 whoopie pie)**

1 box Betty Crocker® SuperMoist® dark chocolate cake mix

½ cup water

½ cup vegetable oil

3 eggs

1 box (4-serving size) chocolate fudge instant pudding and pie filling mix

Filling and Decorations

3 cups chocolate whipped ready-to-spread frosting (from two 12-oz containers)

Halloween sprinkles

1. Heat oven to 350°F. Lightly spray cookie sheets with cooking spray or line with parchment paper.

2. In large bowl, beat cake mix, water, oil, eggs and pudding with electric mixer on low speed until moistened; beat 1 minute on high speed. Drop batter by heaping teaspoonfuls 2 inches apart on cookie sheets, making 34 cookies.

3. Bake 11 to 13 minutes or until set (do not overbake). Cool 2 minutes; remove from cookie sheets to cooling racks. Cool completely, about 15 minutes.

4. For each whoopie pie, spread about 3 tablespoons frosting on bottom of 1 cookie. Top with second cookie, bottom side down. Gently press cookies together. Roll edges of whoopie pies in sprinkles.

1 Serving: Calories 164; Total Fat 11g (Saturated Fat 6g); Sodium 158mg; Total Carbohydrate 14g (Dietary Fiber 1g); Protein 2g **Exchanges:** 1 Other Carbohydrate, 2 Fat **Carbohydrate Choices:** 1

Terrifying Tip

Don't be afraid to make these whoopie pies all year-round using different color sprinkles to reflect the season.

Eyeball Brownie Pops

PREP TIME: 55 Minutes • **START TO FINISH: 2 Hours 55 Minutes** • **36 servings (1 pop)**

Brownie

1 box (1 lb 3.5 oz) chocolate fudge brownie mix

Water, vegetable oil and eggs called for on brownie mix box

Decorations

16 oz vanilla-flavored candy coating (almond bark)

36 paper lollipop sticks

36 green ring-shaped gummy candies or fruit-flavored ring-shaped hard candies

3 brown miniature candy-coated chocolate baking bits

Red food decorating pen or 1 tube (0.68 oz) red decorating gel, if desired

1. Heat oven to 350°F. Grease bottom only of 9-inch square pan with shortening or cooking spray. Make and bake brownies as directed on box for 9-inch pan, using water, oil and eggs. Cool completely.

2. Line cookie sheet with waxed paper. Using cookie scoop, scoop brownies into 36 (1½-inch) balls. Roll between hands to smooth edges; place on cookie sheet. Refrigerate to keep chilled.

3. Line a second cookie sheet with waxed paper. In medium microwavable bowl, microwave candy coating uncovered on Medium (50%) 1 minute, then in 15-second intervals until melted; stir until smooth. Remove several brownie balls at a time from refrigerator. Dip tip of lollipop stick about ½ inch into melted coating and insert stick straight into brownie ball no more than halfway. Dip brownie pop into melted coating to cover, letting excess drip off; place on cookie sheet. Immediately adhere green gummy candies and press brown candies in center for pupils. Let stand until set. Use food decorating pen to draw veins on eyeball pops.

1 Serving: Calories 171; Total Fat 8g (Saturated Fat 4g); Sodium 49mg; Total Carbohydrate 25g (Dietary Fiber 0g); Protein 1g **Exchanges:** 1½ Other Carbohydrate, 1½ Fat **Carbohydrate Choices:** 1½

Terrifying Tip

Use any type of cake decorating writing pen to add details to these brownie pops.

Honey-Pumpkin Dessert Squares

PREP TIME: 25 Minutes • **START TO FINISH: 2 Hours 15 Minutes** • **20 servings**

Crust

- 1 cup all-purpose flour
- 1 cup quick-cooking oats
- ½ cup butter or margarine, softened
- ¼ cup packed brown sugar

Filling

- 2 cans (15 oz each) pumpkin (not pumpkin pie mix)
- 3 eggs
- 1 cup fat-free half-and-half
- ¾ cup honey
- ¾ cup packed brown sugar
- 2 teaspoons pumpkin pie spice
- 1 teaspoon vanilla
- ½ teaspoon salt

Garnish

- ½ cup reduced-fat whipped topping
- 20 candy pumpkins

1. Heat oven to 350°F. In medium bowl, mix crust ingredients with fork until crumbly. Press in bottom of ungreased 13x9-inch pan. Bake 10 minutes.

2. In large bowl, beat filling ingredients with wire whisk or electric mixer on medium speed until blended. Pour over partially baked crust.

3. Bake 55 to 60 minutes or until set and knife inserted in center comes out clean. Cool completely, about 40 minutes.

4. Cut dessert into squares. Serve with whipped topping. Garnish each with candy pumpkin.

1 Serving: Calories 210; Total Fat 5g (Saturated Fat 1.5g); Sodium 135mg; Total Carbohydrate 38g (Dietary Fiber 2g); Protein 3g **Exchanges:** 1 Starch, 1½ Other Carbohydrate, 1 Fat **Carbohydrate Choices:** 2½

Terrifying Tips

Canned pumpkin pie mix contains spices, sugar, water and salt, so it can't be substituted for canned plain pumpkin.

If you don't have candy pumpkins for the garnish, sprinkle a little pumpkin pie spice over the whipped cream.

Pumpkin Spice Malted Milk Ball Brownies

PREP TIME: 15 Minutes • **START TO FINISH: 1 Hour 55 Minutes** • **24 servings (1 brownie)**

Brownie

- 2 oz unsweetened baking chocolate, chopped
- 2 oz semisweet baking chocolate, chopped
- 1 cup butter, softened
- 2 cups sugar
- 3 eggs
- 1 cup all-purpose flour
- ½ cup malted milk powder
- ½ teaspoon salt
- 2 teaspoons vanilla

Frosting and Decorations

- 1 container (1 lb) vanilla creamy ready-to-spread frosting
- 1½ to 2 cups coarsely chopped pumpkin spice malted milk balls

1. Heat oven to 350°F. Grease 13x9-inch pan; lightly flour. In small microwavable bowl, microwave unsweetened and semisweet chocolate uncovered on High 1 minute to 1 minute 45 seconds until softened and chocolate can be stirred smooth.

2. In large bowl, beat butter and sugar with electric mixer on medium speed until light and fluffy. Add eggs, one at a time, beating well after each addition. Stir in melted chocolate. Add flour, malted milk powder, salt and vanilla; beat about 30 seconds or until blended. Spread batter in pan.

3. Bake 35 to 40 minutes or until toothpick inserted in center comes out clean. Cool completely in pan on cooling rack, about 1 hour.

4. Spread frosting over brownies. Sprinkle with malted milk balls, pressing gently to adhere. Cut into 6 rows by 4 rows.

1 Serving: Calories 352; Total Fat 16g (Saturated Fat 9g); Sodium 217mg; Total Carbohydrate 51g (Dietary Fiber 1g); Protein 3g **Exchanges:** 3½ Other Carbohydrate, 2½ Fat **Carbohydrate Choices:** 3½

Terrifying Tip

You can forgo the frosting and gently press the chopped malted milk balls into the batter before baking.

Mini Haunted House

PREP TIME: 1 Hour • **START TO FINISH: 1 Hour** • **8 servings**

12 cinnamon graham cracker rectangles

1 cup chocolate creamy ready-to-spread frosting

½ cup roasted salted pumpkin seeds

Black string licorice, cut into pieces

10 shortbread cookie crisps

¼ cup creamy white ready-to-spread frosting

¼ teaspoon orange gel food color

1 fudge-covered graham cracker

1 orange jelly bean

3 pieces candy corn

1 cup graham cracker crumbs

½ cup chocolate graham cracker crumbs

Candy rocks

8 chocolate cookie sticks and creme, broken

Candy pumpkins

Bone-shaped candy sprinkles

1. On work surface or serving plate, assemble house with 8 cinnamon graham crackers as walls and chocolate frosting as mortar. Frost tops of remaining 4 graham crackers; place on house for roof. Place pumpkin seeds on frosted roof for shingles. Use chocolate frosting to attach licorice pieces to outline house. Use more chocolate frosting to attach shortbread cookie crisps on house for windows. In small bowl, mix white frosting and orange food color. Frost shortbread cookie windows. With small round tip, pipe chocolate frosting for window panes. Pipe RIP on remaining shortbread crisps.

2. Use chocolate frosting to attach fudge-covered graham cracker to house for door. Use frosting to attach jelly bean for door handle and 3 pieces candy corn above door. Sprinkle plain and chocolate crumbs around house. Place candy rocks in front of house for walkway. Use chocolate frosting to stand RIP shortbread next to house. Use chocolate frosting to stand up chocolate cookie sticks around house for fence. Decorate with candy pumpkins and bone sprinkles.

1 Serving: Calories 440; Total Fat 19g (Saturated Fat 5g); Sodium 327mg; Total Carbohydrate 64g (Dietary Fiber 2.5g); Protein 7g **Exchanges:** 2 Starch, 2½ Other Carbohydrate, 3½ Fat **Carbohydrate Choices:** 4½

Terrifying Tip

Engage your kids in this Halloween food craft. Display it on the dining table if you dare!

Cinnamon Roll Bats

PREP TIME: 15 Minutes • **START TO FINISH: 40 Minutes** • **5 rolls**

1 can (17.5 oz) Pillsbury® Grands!® cinnamon rolls with cream cheese icing

5 tablespoons chocolate candy sprinkles

5 chocolate wafer cookies

10 gummy ring candies, ¾ inch

10 miniature candy-coated chocolate baking bits

10 pieces candy corn

5 large or small black gumdrops

1. Heat oven to 350°F. Separate dough into 5 rolls; cut each in half crosswise. For each flying bat, arrange 2 halves, round sides together, on ungreased cookie sheet.

2. Bake 17 to 22 minutes or until golden brown. Reserve 1 tablespoon icing. Frost warm bats with remaining icing. Immediately sprinkle each bat with 1 tablespoon candy sprinkles.

3. With small amount of reserved icing, attach wafer cookie to each bat for head. Use remaining icing and candies to decorate faces as desired.

1 Roll: Calories 530 (Calories from Fat 120); Total Fat 13g (Saturated Fat 6g); Cholesterol 0mg; Sodium 710mg; Total Carbohydrate 96g (Dietary Fiber 2g, Sugars 50g); Protein 6g

Terrifying Tip

Use your imagination to choose other candies to decorate your "bats."

Decadent Dessert Ideas with Leftover Candy

Instead of hauling all of your leftover Halloween candy to the office or hiding it in a cupboard, use these ideas to transform it into amazing treats.

1. Trash Mix

Create the ultimate salty-sweet combo with little pretzel pieces, **gummy candies**, chocolate-covered peanuts and candy corn. Stir in dried fruits and banana chips for a snack your kids will love.

2. Candy Bar Cupcakes

Melt your extra **mini candy bars** and stir into cupcake batter, or top the frosted cupcakes with chopped candy bars.

3. Candy Bar Cheesecake

It's hard to believe that anyone would have leftover **candy bars**, but if you do, chop them up and use them as a topping for cheesecake.

4. Chocolate–Candy Corn Truffles

Instead of shaping chocolate into balls for truffles, spread it into a pan, let it cool and cut it into squares. Then coat the squares in baking cocoa and top with a piece of **candy corn**. You could also top the truffles with any other small, soft Halloween candies.

5. Caramel Brownies

Top brownie batter with **caramel squares** for rich, fudgy brownies with ooey-gooey caramel in the centers.

6. Monster Cookies

Jazz up your oatmeal raisin cookies with **candy-coated chocolate candies**. Mix them into the batter, or place on top of cookies before baking.

Trick-or-Treat Tarts

PREP TIME: 20 Minutes • **START TO FINISH: 3 Hours 40 Minutes** • **24 servings (1 tart)**

Crust

1   box Pillsbury® refrigerated pie crusts, softened as directed on box

Filling

2   bars (2.07 oz each) milk chocolate–covered peanut, caramel and nougat candy

4   oz (half of 8-oz package) cream cheese, softened

2   tablespoons plus 2 teaspoons sugar

1   egg

2   tablespoons sour cream

2   tablespoons creamy peanut butter

Topping

1   tablespoon whipping cream

¼   cup milk chocolate chips

1. Heat oven to 450°F. Unroll pie crusts on work surface. With rolling pin, roll each crust lightly into 12-inch round. With 3-inch round cutter, cut 12 rounds from each crust, rerolling scraps as necessary. Press 1 round in bottom and up side of each of 24 ungreased mini muffin cups, so edges of crusts extend slightly above sides of cups.

2. Bake 5 to 7 minutes or until very light golden brown; cool. Reduce oven temperature to 325°F.

3. Cut candy bars lengthwise in half; cut into ⅛-inch pieces and coarsely chop. Reserve some pieces for garnish; place remaining candy bar pieces in partially baked cups. In small bowl, beat cream cheese and sugar with electric mixer on medium speed until smooth. Beat in egg until well blended. Add sour cream and peanut butter, beating until smooth. Spoon 2 teaspoons cream cheese mixture over candy bar pieces in each cup.

4. Bake 20 to 22 minutes or until center is set. Cool completely, about 30 minutes.

5. In 1-quart saucepan, heat whipping cream until very warm. Remove from heat; stir in chocolate chips until melted and smooth. Spread over top of each tart. Garnish with reserved candy bar pieces. Refrigerate 2 to 3 hours before serving. Cover and refrigerate any remaining tarts.

1 Serving: Calories 140; Total Fat 9g (Saturated Fat 4g); Sodium 125mg; Total Carbohydrate 14g (Dietary Fiber 0g); Protein 2g **Exchanges:** 1 Other Carbohydrate, 1½ Fat **Carbohydrate Choices:** 1

Munchable Mice

1 cup semisweet chocolate chips (6 oz)

2 teaspoons shortening

24 maraschino cherries with stems, well drained

24 Hershey®'s Kisses® milk chocolates, unwrapped

48 sliced almonds

White and red decorating gel, if desired

1. In small microwavable bowl, microwave chocolate chips and shortening uncovered on High 1 minute, stirring once, until softened and chocolate can be stirred smooth. For each mouse, hold 1 cherry by the stem and dip into melted chocolate. Set on waxed paper; press 1 milk chocolate candy onto opposite side of cherry from stem.

2. For ears, insert 2 almonds between cherry and chocolate candy. For eyes, pipe 2 white dots of decorating gel with dots of red decorating gel in centers. Store covered in refrigerator.

1 Serving: Calories 51; Total Fat 3g (Saturated Fat 1g); Sodium 1mg; Total Carbohydrate 8g (Dietary Fiber 1g); Protein 0g **Exchanges:** ½ Other Carbohydrate, ½ Fat **Carbohydrate Choices:** ½

Terrifying Tip

Ease up your party planning by making these adorable almond-eared mice up to 3 days in advance.

Melting Witch Pudding Cups

PREP TIME: 25 Minutes • **START TO FINISH: 25 Minutes** • **8 servings (1 pudding cup)**

Witch Hats Decorations

- ⅓ cup semisweet chocolate chips
- 1 teaspoon shortening
- 8 Bugles® original flavor snacks

Pudding

- 1 box (4-serving size) white chocolate instant pudding and pie filling mix
- 4 cups cold milk
- 1 box (4-serving size) chocolate fudge instant pudding and pie filling mix
- 6 drops green food color

Witch and Broom Decorations

- 8 creme-filled chocolate sandwich cookies or chocolate-covered peppermint patties
- 8 pretzel sticks
- 1 tablespoon Fiber One® original bran cereal or chow mein noodles, pieces broken in half
- 16 gummy worm candies

1. In small microwavable bowl, microwave chocolate chips and shortening on High 1 to 2 minutes or until melted; stir until smooth. To make witch hats, dip Bugles snacks into melted chocolate, letting excess drip off. Place point up on plate. Let stand until set.

2. Make white chocolate pudding with 2 cups of the milk as directed on box. Make chocolate fudge pudding with remaining 2 cups milk. Stir green food color into white chocolate pudding.

3. For each pudding cup, spoon 2 tablespoons green pudding into 4-ounce cup; top with 2 tablespoons chocolate fudge pudding. Repeat with each flavor to form 4 layers. With spoon handle, gently swirl top 2 layers. Insert cookie in pudding; top with witch hat. Insert pretzel stick into pudding with cereal pieces at base to look like broom. Insert ends of gummy candies into pudding to look like legs.

1 Serving: Calories 320; Total Fat 8g (Saturated Fat 4g); Sodium 510mg; Total Carbohydrate 55g (Dietary Fiber 2g); Protein 6g **Exchanges:** 1 Starch, 2 Other Carbohydrate, ½ Low-Fat Milk, 1 Fat **Carbohydrate Choices:** 3½

Terrifying Tips

Substitute purchased swirled pudding snacks for the white chocolate and chocolate fudge pudding combination. Assemble the witches directly on top of the pudding cups.

Make the dipped Bugles® a bit ahead of time. Then, assemble one example for the kids and let them make the rest.

Halloween Buddies

PREP TIME: 15 Minutes • **START TO FINISH: 15 Minutes** • **30 servings (¼ cup each)**

4½ cups Corn Chex® cereal

½ cup semisweet chocolate chips (3 oz)

¼ cup peanut butter

2 tablespoons butter or margarine

½ teaspoon vanilla

¾ cup powdered sugar

1 cup candy corn

1 cup salted cocktail peanuts

1. Into large bowl, measure cereal; set aside.

2 In 1-quart microwavable bowl, microwave chocolate chips, peanut butter and butter uncovered on High 30 seconds; stir. Microwave about 15 seconds longer or until mixture can be stirred smooth. Stir in vanilla. Pour mixture over cereal, stirring until evenly coated. Pour into 1-gallon resealable food-storage plastic bag.

3. Add powdered sugar. Seal bag; shake until well coated. Add candy corn and peanuts; shake to mix. Spread on waxed paper to cool. Store in airtight container in refrigerator.

1 Serving: Calories 120; Total Fat 5g (Saturated Fat 1.5g); Sodium 100mg; Total Carbohydrate 16g (Dietary Fiber 0g); Protein 2g **Exchanges:** 1 Starch, 1 Fat **Carbohydrate Choices:** 1

Terrifying Tip

This recipe can easily be doubled—just use twice the ingredient amounts, the microwave times and the size of the bag!

Coconut-Covered Ice Cream Ghosts

PREP TIME: 20 Minutes • **START TO FINISH: 1 Hour 20 Minutes** • **8 servings (1 ghost)**

Ice Cream Filling

1 pint (2 cups) vanilla ice cream

1 pint (2 cups) chocolate ice cream

Decorations

2 cups shredded coconut

16 semisweet chocolate chips

1. Line cookie sheet with waxed paper. With ½-cup ice cream scoop, scoop 4 balls of vanilla ice cream and 4 balls of chocolate ice cream onto cookie sheet. Freeze 30 minutes or until firm.

2. Working quickly, roll each vanilla ice cream ball in coconut, coating well. Repeat with chocolate ice cream balls, coating well. Return to cookie sheet; freeze 30 minutes or until firm.

3. Press 2 chocolate chips into each ice cream ball to look like ghost eyes. Freeze until serving time.

1 Serving: Calories 251; Total Fat 15g (Saturated Fat 11g); Sodium 96mg; Total Carbohydrate 28g (Dietary Fiber 3g); Protein 4g **Exchanges:** 2 Other Carbohydrate, 3 Fat **Carbohydrate Choices:** 2

Terrifying Tip

Freeze the cookie sheet before you begin scooping ice cream for this recipe. This step will contribute to the quick freeze needed to set the ice cream balls.

Scarecrow Ice Cream Cones

PREP TIME: 20 Minutes • **START TO FINISH: 1 Hour 50 Minutes** • **12 servings (1 scarecrow)**

Ice Cream Filling

1½ quarts (6 cups) vanilla ice cream

Decorations

4 cups Honey Nut Chex® cereal

1 tube (4.25 oz) white decorator icing

12 pieces candy corn

24 brown, green and blue candy-coated chocolate candies

1 cup thin pretzel sticks (2¼ inch), broken in half

12 sugar-style ice cream cones with pointed ends

1. Line cookie sheet with waxed paper. Using ice cream scoop or ½-cup measuring cup, scoop 12 mounds of ice cream onto cookie sheet. Quickly shape into balls. Freeze 30 minutes or until firm.

2. Place cereal in resealable food-storage plastic bag; seal bag and coarsely crush with rolling pin or flat side of meat mallet. Remove ice cream balls from freezer; roll in crushed cereal until well coated. Return to cookie sheet. Freeze 1 hour or until firm.

3. Just before serving and using icing to secure candies, decorate each ice cream ball with 1 piece candy corn for nose, 2 chocolate candies for eyes and 8 to 10 pretzel pieces for hair. Top each ice cream ball with ice cream cone hat.

1 Serving: Calories 312; Total Fat 12g (Saturated Fat 6g); Sodium 205mg; Total Carbohydrate 46g (Dietary Fiber 0.5g); Protein 5g **Exchanges:** 1 Starch, 2 Other Carbohydrate, 2 Fat **Carbohydrate Choices:** 3

Terrifying Tip

These can be made with any combination of ice cream and cereal. To make a grown-up version, use coffee-flavored ice cream and cover in chopped chocolate-covered coffee beans.

Witch Hat Ice Cream Sandwiches

PREP TIME: 35 Minutes • START TO FINISH: 2 Hours 5 Minutes • 12 servings (1 ice cream sandwich)

Cookies

1 pouch (1 lb 1.5 oz) sugar cookie mix

⅓ cup butter or margarine, softened

1 egg

Ice Cream Filling and Decorations

3 cups mint chocolate chip ice cream

1 cup dark cocoa candy melts

Candy sprinkles, if desired

1. Heat oven to 375°F. In medium bowl, stir cookie mix, butter and egg until soft dough forms. On lightly floured surface, roll dough to ¼-inch thickness. Cut with 3- or 4-inch witch hat–shaped cookie cutter. On ungreased cookie sheet, place cutouts 1 inch apart.

2. Bake 9 to 11 minutes or until edges are light golden brown. Cool 2 minutes; remove from cookie sheets to cooling racks. Cool completely, about 30 minutes.

3. For each ice cream sandwich, press about ¼ cup ice cream between 2 cookies. Wrap individually in plastic wrap. Freeze until firm, about 1 hour, or until serving time. Melt candy coating as directed on package; brush over one side of each ice cream sandwich. Decorate with sprinkles. Freeze until chocolate is set.

1 Serving: Calories 420; Total Fat 20g (Saturated Fat 12g); Sodium 164mg; Total Carbohydrate 54g (Dietary Fiber 0g); Protein 3g **Exchanges:** ½ Starch, 3 Other Carbohydrate, 4 Fat **Carbohydrate Choices:** 3½

Terrifying Tip

This treat can be made with any of your favorite flavors of cookie mixes or ice creams. Try using peanut butter cookie mix and peanut butter cup ice cream.

Pear Ghosts

PREP TIME: 10 Minutes • START TO FINISH: 10 Minutes • 6 servings (1 pear ghost)

1 **container (1 lb) vanilla creamy ready-to-spread frosting**

6 **craft sticks (flat wooden sticks with round ends)**

6 **firm ripe Bartlett pears**

12 **miniature semisweet chocolate chips or small candies**

1 **tablespoon semisweet chocolate chips**

1. Spoon half of the frosting into medium microwavable bowl. Microwave on High for 30 seconds. Stir in remaining frosting.

2. Insert 1 wooden stick into each pear near stem. Holding each pear by stick, dip in warm frosting. Holding pear over frosting, spoon additional frosting over pear until completely coated; let excess drip back into bowl. Place on waxed paper. Press 2 miniature chocolate chips into frosting on each pear for eyes.

3. Place 1 tablespoon chocolate chips in resealable freezer plastic bag. Microwave on medium (50%) 20 seconds. Gently squeeze bag. Microwave an additional 10 seconds until chocolate is smooth. Cut off tiny corner of bag. Squeeze bag to pipe mouth on each ghost.

1 Serving: Calories 435; Total Fat 12g (Saturated Fat 10g); Sodium 5mg; Total Carbohydrate 81g (Dietary Fiber 4g); Protein 1g **Exchanges:** 3½ Starch, 2 Fruit, 5½ Other Carbohydrate, 2½ Fat **Carbohydrate Choices:** 5½

metric conversion guide

Volume

U.S. Units	Canadian Metric	Australian Metric
¼ teaspoon	1 mL	1 ml
½ teaspoon	2 mL	2 ml
1 teaspoon	5 mL	5 ml
1 tablespoon	15 mL	20 ml
¼ cup	50 mL	60 ml
⅓ cup	75 mL	80 ml
½ cup	125 mL	125 ml
⅔ cup	150 mL	170 ml
¾ cup	175 mL	190 ml
1 cup	250 mL	250 ml
1 quart	1 liter	1 liter
1½ quarts	1.5 liters	1.5 liters
2 quarts	2 liters	2 liters
2½ quarts	2.5 liters	2.5 liters
3 quarts	3 liters	3 liters
4 quarts	4 liters	4 liters

Weight

U.S. Units	Canadian Metric	Australian Metric
1 ounce	30 grams	30 grams
2 ounces	55 grams	60 grams
3 ounces	85 grams	90 grams
4 ounces (¼ pound)	115 grams	125 grams
8 ounces (½ pound)	225 grams	225 grams
16 ounces (1 pound)	455 grams	500 grams
1 pound	455 grams	½ kilogram

Measurements

Inches	Centimeters
1	2.5
2	5.0
3	7.5
4	10.0
5	12.5
6	15.0
7	17.5
8	20.5
9	23.0
10	25.5
11	28.0
12	30.5
13	33.0

Temperatures

Fahrenheit	Celsius
32°	0°
212°	100°
250°	120°
275°	140°
300°	150°
325°	160°
350°	180°
375°	190°
400°	200°
425°	220°
450°	230°
475°	240°
500°	260°

Note: The recipes in this cookbook have not been developed or tested using metric measures. When converting recipes to metric, some variations in quality may be noted.

Recipe Testing and Calculating Nutrition Information

RECIPE TESTING:

- Large eggs and 2% milk were used unless otherwise indicated.

- Fat-free, low-fat, low-sodium or lite products were not used unless indicated.

- No nonstick cookware and bakeware were used unless otherwise indicated. No dark-colored, black or insulated bakeware was used.

- When a pan is specified, a metal pan was used; a baking dish or pie plate means ovenproof glass was used.

- An electric hand mixer was used for mixing only when mixer speeds are specified.

CALCULATING NUTRITION:

- The first ingredient was used wherever a choice is given, such as $\frac{1}{3}$ cup sour cream or plain yogurt.

- The first amount was used wherever a range is given, such as 3- to $3\frac{1}{2}$-pound whole chicken.

- The first serving number was used wherever a range is given, such as 4 to 6 servings.

- "If desired" ingredients were not included.

- Only the amount of a marinade or frying oil that is absorbed was included.

Index

Complete your cookbook library with these *Betty Crocker* titles

Betty Crocker 30-Minute Meals for Diabetes

Betty Crocker 300 Calorie Cookbook

Betty Crocker Baking Basics

Betty Crocker Baking for Today

Betty Crocker's Best Bread Machine Cookbook

Betty Crocker's Best-Loved Recipes

Betty Crocker The Big Book of Cookies

Betty Crocker The Big Book of Cupcakes

Betty Crocker The Big Book of Slow Cooker, Casseroles & More

Betty Crocker The Big Book of Weeknight Dinners

Betty Crocker Bisquick® II Cookbook

Betty Crocker Bisquick® Impossibly Easy Pies

Betty Crocker Bisquick® to the Rescue

Betty Crocker Christmas Cookbook

Betty Crocker's Cook Book for Boys and Girls

Betty Crocker Cookbook, 11th Edition— The **BIG RED** *Cookbook*®

Betty Crocker Cookbook, Bridal Edition

Betty Crocker's Cooking Basics

Betty Crocker's Cooky Book, Facsimile Edition

Betty Crocker Country Cooking

Betty Crocker Decorating Cakes and Cupcakes

Betty Crocker's Diabetes Cookbook

Betty Crocker's Easy Slow Cooker Dinners

Betty Crocker's Eat and Lose Weight

Betty Crocker Fix-with-a-Mix Desserts

Betty Crocker Gluten-Free Cooking

Betty Crocker Grilling Made Easy

Betty Crocker Healthy Heart Cookbook

Betty Crocker's Indian Home Cooking

Betty Crocker's Italian Cooking

Betty Crocker's Kids Cook!

Betty Crocker Living with Cancer Cookbook

Betty Crocker Low-Carb Lifestyle Cookbook

Betty Crocker's Low-Fat, Low-Cholesterol Cooking Today

Betty Crocker Money Saving Meals

Betty Crocker More Slow Cooker Recipes

Betty Crocker's New Cake Decorating

Betty Crocker One-Dish Meals

Betty Crocker's Picture Cook Book, Facsimile Edition

Betty Crocker's Quick & Easy Cookbook

Betty Crocker's Slow Cooker Cookbook

Betty Crocker Ultimate Bisquick® Cookbook

Betty Crocker's Ultimate Cake Mix Cookbook

Betty Crocker's Vegetarian Cooking

Betty Crocker Why It Works